The Enchanted World

DWARFS

The Enchanted World

DWARFS

by Tim Appenzeller
and the Editors of Time-Life Books

The Content

Time-Life Books · Alexandria, Virginia

Chapter One

Stern Sons of the Earth

One morning not long after the sea-roving Norse colonized the Faeroe Islands in the northernmost reaches of the Atlantic, a settler grasped his peat knife and headed for a bog to cut fuel for the winter. Mists coiled up from the fjords and inlets that indented the coastline, and the thin mantle of grass and moss that cloaked the pitched flanks of the island squelched under his feet. High, rain-slicked cliffs of black basalt loomed before him, and he remembered tales of dwarfs. The tales told of a second race populating these lonely islands, a race that seldom was seen. Its members revealed themselves in wisps of smoke curling from rockfalls where they had hidden their tiny forges, in piles of ash that appeared at the bases of crags—the sweepings of minute smithies—and in frantic footsteps that sometimes could be heard through the mist as a dwarf sought to conceal himself from a human intruder. But in all his autumn forays to cut peat, the islander had noticed nothing. This time, however, was

different. The path wound through a litter of boulders, then skirted the base of a cliff. A cleft that he did not remember yawned on the face of the rock, and he saw an orange glow flickering on the fractured stone. Smoke billowed from the top of the cleft, and clattering, hissing noises like those of a smithy issued from the opening.

The man inched along the cliff base to the mouth of the cavern, hardly breathing. He risked a look, then stared transfixed. There, deep in the rock, was the source of the glow—a well-stoked forge that sent a whirlwind of flame twisting toward the cathedral-like ceiling of the cleft. And silhouetted against the blaze were three tiny figures, no higher than a man's waist but casting shadows that reared dark and menacing on the wall of rock behind them.

Only with difficulty could the peat cutter pick out the dwarf smiths from among the stones of their rock-built forge. Their skin and aprons were the same sooty gray as the stone; their bodies were as squat and rounded as heaped boulders; their features were as coarse and craggy as living rock. But gradually, peering through the shadows and firelight, he distinguished their separate activities.

One plied the bellows, lofting a cloud

of sparks with each stroke. Another used tongs to hold a glowing scrap of iron steady on the ringing anvil, now and then stabbing the metal into the fire to reheat it. The third, his corded arms glistening, wielded the hammer.

The pace of their work was superhuman: The dwarfs completed piece after piece with a few hammer blows, plunging each into a vat of water to quench and toughen it, releasing clouds of steam and an evil sizzle. And beside them grew a pile of objects that, to the poor peat cutter's eyes, was as fine as any Viking hoard. There were plowshares and scythes, stoutly wrought; there were daggers as keen and liquidly gleaming as the best Danish steel; there were smoothly rounded kettles and caldrons and even a few finely fashioned trinkets of silver filigree.

The dwarfs' power over lifeless metal seemed magical, and the man forgot himself in wonderment. Carelessly, he let his peat knife slip to the ground. At the sound, the dwarfs dropped their work; the cave fell silent, and the flames died down. They turned fleshy faces toward the opening of the cavern, their cave dwellers' eyes pained and blinking in the pale daylight.

Then one of the dwarfs bent to sort through the pile of smithcraft. He selected a knife, as long as a man's forearm and glinting in the glow of the embers. The man drew back in fear—until he saw that the dwarf held the knife by the blade.

Bandy-legged and hunchbacked, the dwarf scuttled quick as a spider across the rubbled cavern floor. With a glance that mingled shyness and a hint of warning, he thrust the knife into the man's grasp.

The islander marveled at the blade, so bright and capable next to the stained and pitted iron of his own peat knife, a product of the village smithy. When he turned to gaze again at the stunted artisans, his eyes met featureless stone. The dwarfs were closed in the dark rock once again.

That was the man's one encounter with dwarfs. In all the autumns that followed, the cliff never again opened to reveal its denizens. But he cherished the blade and passed it on to his children, for it never rusted or dulled, and it was a rare souvenir of a hidden race.

Those were days when dwarfs dwelled throughout northern Europe, wherever men and women lived close to the land. Inhabiting rocks, caves, mounds and even forgotten crannies in farmhouses and barns, they passed their lives in ways as earthy and arduous as their peasant neighbors. They were an elfin countryfolk, and their powers were those of a supernatural peasantry: They were uncannily adept at crafts, preternaturally wise in matters of the seasons and the soil.

Their names varied from land to land and region to region. The British Isles had their goblins, knackers and leprechauns, Germany its *Erdleute* and *Stillevolk*, and Scandinavia its trolls and *bergfolk* and *huldrefolk*. But their kinship to the earth, their matchless skills and their stunted stature were universal.

They shared another trait, too, one suggested by the German term *Stillevolk*, or "Quiet People": They were a reclusive race. Although dwarfs were intimately entwined in the lives of the countryfolk of some lands, the interactions were a matter of secret cooperation or furtive mischief: Humans and dwarfs rarely met face to face. Even in the Faeroes – hostile, treeless and swept by Arctic winds, peopled only by a few settlers who eked out a living by raising sheep, gathering seabirds' eggs and fishing the gray Atlantic swell – dwarfs kept clear of their mortal neighbors.

As befitted a people so closely allied to the earth, their presence was most often evident on the face of the landscape or the breath of the wind. A patch of unusual lushness on a grassy hillside might indicate the underground fires of a dwarf's forge or oven, warming the soil above it and quickening vegetative growth. Within the earth itself, a tapping sound that came from a region untunneled by mortal miners might betray the activity of a mining party of dwarfs. And in Scandinavia, echoes cast back from stony mountainsides were known in the Norse language as *dvergamal* – "voice of the dwarf." Dwarfs, perhaps amusing themselves, were said to cause the echo by mimicking any sound heard in their domain. But they melted into the rocks long before a human intruder could draw near enough to spot them.

Yet it was not always so. Long before the peat cutter stared openmouthed at the rock-dwelling smiths as if at members of some long-lost tribe, dwarfs had mingled with the first, heroic mortals as equals. And earlier still, before newly shaped mortals rubbed the sleep from their eyes and set about gaining dominion over the young earth, dwarfs had known days of unequaled power and glory.

The secretive smiths of the Faeroes represented a race that had suffered a long decline. They were as old as the rocks they inhabited, and from that ancient bond with the earth had come mundane wisdom and an intimacy with earthly mysteries. Yet age had also weakened their stock, and they had faltered and retreated before the brazen mortals who inherited the world.

Vestiges of their splendid past remained: It was known that dwarfs sometimes hoarded within their mountains and grottoes ancient treasures forged by their ancestors, and that they practiced magic of incalculable age. Inevitably, mortals tried to fathom the heritage of their mysterious neighbors. But accounts of the distant days when dwarfs consorted with the great powers that shaped the world were sketchy and contradictory, having filtered down from the earliest generations of mortals – after originating, perhaps, with the dwarfs themselves.

The only written accounts of the primeval dwarfs came from Iceland, that land of fire and ice on the far fringe of the northern world, where literary men of the Middle Ages elaborated fragmentary tales of the dawning days of creation into sweeping narratives of first things. Known as Eddas, these accounts reveal dwarfs in their earliest state, as smiths to the gods and figures of titanic powers. They had none of their successors' shyness, but were as brash and swaggering as their station warranted – perhaps more so.

After all, according to the Eddas, the dwarfs sprang into being close on the heels of the gods, and they took shape from the same primordial stuff as the planet's rocks, mountains and seas. The tale of the origin of dwarfs is one and the same as the dawning of the earth.

The Eddic accounts begin before creation, when the cosmos was claimed on one side by fire, on the other by ice, and between them by a great emptiness. In that void roiled clouds of icy vapor exhaled by the realm of frosts, suffused with the flickering glow cast by the region of flame. And in the midst of that gulf, at the first moment of creation, a finger of ice met a tongue of flame.

Life kindled at the touch and fed on the crystalline droplets of water that sparkled in the void as the ice melted. Soon a form swelled in the region between fire and ice: a rude giant, uncouth and irascible. The ancient bards called him Ymir, and he had a boundless, self-sufficient vitality. After his titanic struggle into existence, he slept, and from the rank sweat that beaded in his armpit two other giants took shape—a man and a woman—and a third giant was spawned by Ymir's feet as they kicked and scuffed in uneasy dreams. Ymir's offspring quickly multiplied, giving rise to the frost giants, the first race to populate the cosmos.

But the giants had little time to lord it over the void. Strife came early in the cosmos, and strife was the force that gave birth to a tortured and flawed world, a place where summer was a brief, bright respite from endless cold and gloom, where arable land lay in a narrow strip between granite mountains and fathomless fjords. The strife also gave birth to that world's earliest inhabitants, the dwarfs.

Here is how it happened: First an enormous cow took shape from the meltwater as flames continued to lick at the glacial wastes. From her udders flowed a tide of nourishment for the frost giants, and she took sustenance from the ice itself. As she licked it, her raspy tongue gradually uncovered a comely figure: the god Buri, mysteriously entombed in the ice before time began. He sprang to life in the mild air of creation, and like Ymir, he was father and mother both to a crop of descendants.

Buri's spawn was a brood of gods, and as these new beings grew in power and vitality, they began to feel themselves the rightful masters of the universe. With one accord, they fell on Ymir. Mites on his vast form, the gods bit his sinews and tore at his throbbing arteries, and at last Ymir vomited a stream of blood—drowning all but two of the frost giants—and died.

Then the enterprising gods divided the spoils, using the parts of Ymir's body to fashion a world over which to reign. They stripped the flesh from the carcass and spread it in carpets of soft and fertile land. They strewed his teeth and shattered bones across the land as boulders and crags. And from Ymir's spine and the long bones that remained unbroken, they heaped up ramparts and mountain chains. Then they confined the dark, foaming blood in seas and bays and landlocked lakes, and over the entire new-created earth they set the high dome of Ymir's skull, as the sky that bounds the world and separates it from the void beyond. Cling-

Norsemen said that the world was created from the sundered body of the frost
giant Ymir. Out of his earth-corpse squirmed maggoty creatures, blessed by
the gods with human wit and form; thus were the first dwarfs born.

ing to that great arch of bone were whorled masses of gray — tatters of Ymir's brain, transmuted by the ingenuity of the gods to clouds. To complete their creation, the gods snagged stray sparks from the realm of fire and cast them into the sky to form sun, moon and stars.

Within the soil, life quickened and began to squirm: the dwarfs. As maggots spring from decaying flesh, say the Eddas, so the dwarfs took form within the vast landscape of Ymir's corpse. Children of the earth, they were at first as featureless as earthworms. But the gods high in Asgard, the fortress they had built for themselves, sensed the stirrings far below. They fostered the dwarfs, endowing them with wit and speech and a physical form that was a squat parody of their own godly shapes. The gods left most of the dwarfs within the clefts and folds and grottoes of the young earth. But they plucked out four dwarfs — the broadest of limb and the stoutest of shoulder — and set one at each corner of the sky, to hold the great dome steady for as long as creation endured.

Only when the rest of creation was in place did the first mortals appear, and their advent was a matter of happenstance. Wandering the lonely shores of the young earth, the gods noticed a pair of stately ash trees, growing just behind the beach. To pass the time, they cut down the trees, carved the trunks in their own likeness and endowed the wooden figures with life, sense and motion. When the gods went on their way, they left behind them on the strand a man and a woman, the first of the race of mortals. That race's time would come, but during the first ages, the descendants of the pair counted for little more than the deer in the forest and the fish in the sea.

No doubt the Eddic account contains a large measure of fantasy, but in the matter of dwarfs, its implied truths seem sound. The kinship of dwarfs to the soil and their link to death and decay is borne out in tale after tale. The primeval dwarfs were earth dwellers, corpse gray in color, and shunners of daylight, which could turn them to stone. Stone was their womb as well as their habitat, and one account claimed that these first dwarfs, who numbered no women among them, perpetuated their

race by fashioning new dwarfs from rock.

Humble though their physical make-up was, the same grandeur implicit in their role as sustainers of the sky pervades every one of their legendary deeds. Living in a realm of dark rock and flickering volcanic flame, moving through underground passageways as easily as fish course the water and birds ride the wind, they were guardians and master manipulators of the earth's mineral riches.

Their talents with metal and gemstones found application far beyond their subterranean kingdom. The Scandinavian pantheon was devoted to war and luxury, and naturally looked to the dwarfs for arms and adornment. Yet such was the dwarfs' awareness of their unique gifts that although they could not match the gods in might, they did not answer to the gods' orders. Only cajoling and flattery would induce them to exercise their skills.

To one god, a subtle-tongued trickster named Loki, blandishments came easily. And he once had great need of this ability, for he angered Thor, the bluff and potent thunder god, and could make recompense only with a dwarf-forged treasure.

One evening, as he darted through the great palace of Asgard in search of diversion, Loki noticed that the door to the chamber of Sif, Thor's wife, was ajar. He could not resist: He slipped in and gazed down at the sleeping goddess, her shoulders and breasts awash in shimmering blond tresses. Devilry swept over Loki; smirking, he drew his dagger, gathered up Sif's hair and sheared it to the scalp. The goddess still slept, her head covered with unsightly stubble, while Loki scattered the tresses about the chamber and, still chortling, slipped out the door.

Seeing his radiant bride despoiled, Thor was beside himself, and he guessed the culprit. He caught Loki just as the trickster tried to slink past him with an ingratiating smile. His brow black with rage, Thor threatened punishment. But Loki promised to make amends, and Thor, though dubious, released him.

Loki now was in need of skill beyond any to be found in Asgard. From the gates of the fortress, a slender bridge as bright and tenuous as a rainbow—the form in which it was said to be visible to mortals—spanned the gulf between Asgard and Midgard, the middle earth, where dwarfs and the first mortals dwelled. Swift as a sparkle of sunshine, the god sped down the bridge and over the rude camps of mortals to the stony northern realm of the dwarfs.

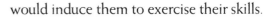

The god hovered above a landscape honeycombed with caverns and pitted with glacial potholes, many of them cupping gray ponds. In the northern half-light, curls of smoke rose from fires hidden in the pits and caverns. At last Loki recognized a landmark and dropped toward the darkling landscape.

Alighting, he picked his way down a winding corridor, led on by the distant clang of forges and the flicker of firelight. The passage opened into a vast underground chamber, a mammoth workshop in which the air billowed with smoke and the glow of countless fires was reflected by treasures that littered the floor and spilled from niches in the cavern walls. The glittering objects were the products of the dwarfs' restless ingenuity.

There were pendants and brooches ornamented with silver-filigree designs of swirling battle scenes and borders of endlessly intertwined serpents. There were sinuous armbands of gold so fine that it seemed to smolder in the firelight. There were helmets of iron and bronze, given the fearsome likeness of human faces with heavy nose guards and jutting bronze brows; the metal was inlaid with traceries in glossy niello showing ranked men-at-arms and soldiers in single combat.

Here and there stood a broadax, the blade flaring to a foot or more in width—a weapon so stout that a warrior would need both hands to wield it. And there were bright swords, the flats of their blades swirling with silvery patterns like sheafs of grain—the ghostly tracery of the multitude of iron bars that were interwoven and flattened during their making. Loki gazed about him in wonder and greed, but he sought a treasure more wondrous still.

Far in the smoky depths of the cavern, he caught sight of the two brothers known as Ivaldi's sons, smiths especially gifted even among the dwarf race. He hurried over to them, and they turned sooty faces from their work to gaze with curiosity at the intruder. tall and slender and aglow with the light of a higher sphere. "Someone has shorn Sif's hair," said Loki, neglecting to explain just how this had happened, "and the gods have sent me to see if it lies within your powers to replace it."

Finding little to interest them in such a task, the dwarf smiths shrugged and turned back to their forge. "The feat will add to your renown among the gods," continued Loki, and he expanded on the high esteem in which the gods already held the smiths, and the greater glories his own praise could bring them.

In the end, his flattery won them over. They conferred, then set to work. One of the brothers heaped charcoal into the furnace and pumped a pigskin bellows until flames rose in a furious storm; the other sorted his stock of metals, choosing slender rods of the finest gold. When the coals had reached just the right temperature, the second dwarf heated the gold; then, his fat hands working faster than Loki's eyes could follow, he divided and drew the gold into a sheaf of threads so fine that the metal was as silky and as pliant as the hair of a goddess. "They are the equal of Sif's own," said the smith as he handed the golden skeins to Loki, the metal still

Earth-bred and -bound, dwarfs mastered the mundane elements. The first members of this stunted race chiseled progeny from stone, for there were no women among them.

In the days when a god might still visit lower realms—as the trickster god Loki
did once in search of dwarf-wrought treasures—the bridge from heaven to
earth was visible as an arc of brilliant hues. Mortals called it the rainbow.

warm from the forge. "When she touches them to her scalp, they will take root and grow like living hair."

Loki was speechless with amazement. He saw that the dwarfs had powers that far exceeded the shaping and hammering of metal. But once again the dwarfs were stoking and fanning their forge to a roaring blaze. Said one smith: "The forge is hot, and we are hungry for renown. We will show you what we can do."

In a blaze of sparks and metal scorched to white heat, marvels took shape on the dwarfs' anvil. The first seemed no more than a flimsy assemblage of iron wires and panels, and Loki sneered at it. But the smith silenced him. He spread the panels and straightened the wires, and like a gathering thundercloud, the framework grew in size and substance until a vast warship, tight-planked and tall-masted, its sails billowing, loomed in the smoke of the cavern. The dwarf ran his hand along the keel, and in an instant the planks and mast and rigging dissolved, and the paltry collection of iron scraps clattered to the cavern floor. "The ship's name is *Skidbladnir*," said the dwarf, "and it will fit in your pocket. But when it is unfurled, it will hold the entire host of gods, with all their weapons, and it will bear them over land and sea, never lacking for a favorable wind."

Then the dwarfs turned back to the forge and wrought a final wonder. Beaten from a single block of iron, it was a spear, seemingly like any other. But it, too, had a name, expressive of its magic. The dwarfs called it Gungnir and said that it was a spear suited to a god, for no wind or contrary spirit could turn it from its mark.

Although he was dazzled by the dwarfs' displays of skill, a cunning light had begun to dance in Loki's eyes. The treasures he would carry back to Asgard would win him not only Thor's forgiveness but the gratitude of all the gods. And he guessed that by playing on dwarfish pride, he could elicit a second crop of matchless objects to distribute among the pantheon.

With a flurry of praise and thanks, Loki gathered up the golden tresses, the folding ship and the magic spear and hurried up the corridor into the twilight. He climbed over a rubble-strewn ridge and gazed down into a pothole, where a forge glowed at the edge of a still lake. Then he sped down the slope into the pit, shouting his challenge: "O dwarfs, match these treasures, if you can."

His hearers, brothers named Brokk and Sindri, were as famed for their smithcraft as Ivaldi's sons, and their self-esteem was vast. The squat pair folded their arms across their leather-aproned bellies and faced the eager god, his arms full of bright marvels. "And if, in the judgment of the gods, we surpass them?" asked Brokk.

"I wager my head that you will not," said Loki, recklessly calculating that dwarfs, in their pride, would seize any opportunity to gain power over a god.

"Done!" said Brokk. He gathered charcoal and coarse lumps of iron, rods of gold and a great, stiff pigskin. Then he and his brother huddled close to the forge, their stout, humped forms dark against a dazzle of flame. As Sindri's sinewy arm flashed up and down in a blur of hammerstrokes, Loki could see nothing of their work. But he grew less confident that the creations of Ivaldi's sons would prove the best.

Fearing that his wager had been rash, he resorted to a power all gods possessed — that of changing shape. He shriveled and dwindled, sprouting spindly legs and dry, crackling wings, then took to the air as a horsefly. He settled on the back of Brokk's hand as it plunged and rose on the handle of the bellows, and bit viciously through the sweat-slicked skin. The dwarf cursed as a bead of blood welled from the bite, but he did not break his rhythm.

Loki took wing again and buzzed through the welter of smoke as the brothers set aside their first treasure: a golden-bristled boar named Gullinbursti, formed of pigskin and gold wire but endowed with magical life, that stood snorting in the pool of light shed by its luminous bristles, awaiting a rider.

As the brothers began to forge their second wonder, Loki dived again, this time making for Brokk's streaming neck. Again he alighted and bit; again the dwarf cursed but, mindful of his brother's urgings to pump steadily, did not lift a hand from the bellows. And again Sindri drew a treasure from the forge: an armband, gracefully shaped of fine gold. As it cooled, Sindri knelt over it. He named it Draupnir and muttered spells that would cause it to spawn eight new rings, as fine as itself, every ninth night — a priceless harvest of gold. Loki, still buzzing and darting, listened and was frantic with apprehension.

For their final creation, Brokk and Sindri heaved a lump of iron into the coals. Loki's unease subsided at the sight of the humble metal. But Sindri's hammer blows set up a greater din than ever, and Brokk's broad back was knotted with strain as he worked the bellows. Loki, desperate now, darted through the hot blast of the forge and nipped Brokk on the skin of one eyelid. Blood trickled into the dwarf's eye; he lifted a hand to brush away the blood and the maddening fly, and at once the bellows went flat. Sindri swore at Brokk and declared his work spoiled, and Loki flitted behind a boulder and strode into view again in his usual form. As he emerged, the dwarfs, wielding great tongs, hefted a stout, short-handled hammer from the forge to the quenching vat. The god smiled with satisfaction at the crude appearance of the dwarfs' culminating work.

"Do not scorn it," said Brokk, who had noticed Loki's smirk. "It is a little short in the handle, because of a horsefly that bit me while I worked the bellows. But it has wondrous traits: It will shatter whatever it is hurled at, will never break and will always return to the thrower's hand. It is called Mjollnir, and it is a weapon for Thor in his battles against the giants."

Feeling that his triumph was certain, and eager to savor it, Brokk followed the crestfallen Loki up the steep and tremulous bridge from the middle earth to the high ramparts of Asgard. There Loki presented the smithwork of Ivaldi's sons, and Brokk his rival treasures. Sif was speechless with delight as the golden tresses restored her beauty, and all the other godly recipients marveled at their gifts. But, with one accord, the gods pro-

Pounding anvils and murmuring mighty spells, dwarf brothers, Ivaldi's sons,

fashioned a warship that could carry the gods yet fold to fit in a pocket.

nounced the hammer that Brokk bestowed on Thor the most wonderful of all.

Brokk's pallid cheeks flushed, and his eyes glittered with pleasure at the thought of avenging himself on the god who had scoffed at his brother's handiwork. Ready to claim Loki's head, he fingered the pommel of the dagger that was belted to his thick waist. But Loki, resourceful as always, declared that the dwarf was entitled only to his head, and to no other part of him, and therefore had no right to sever his neck. By this stroke of cunning, the dwarf was de-

prived of his revenge; he contented himself with silencing Loki by piercing his lips with an awl and binding them together with stout thread. Warmed by the gods' praise and gratitude, he retired to his smoky pothole in the middle earth.

The high place that such ancestral dwarfs held in the Eddas was not due merely to their prowess as artisans—a prowess more closely akin to wizardry than craftsmanship. The same communion with the earth that gave them preternatural abilities in the shaping of metals engendered more exalted powers: The dwarfs, in fact, were privy to secrets of the universe hidden even from the gods. For all their mightiness and bluster, the gods were vulnerable to forces of chaos that constantly threatened their orderly, three-tiered cosmos: Asgard above, Midgard below and Niflheim, the chill abode of the dead, lower still. At the fringes of this ranked and structured universe lurked giants and monsters, creatures of riot and disorder. Because dwarfs were themselves linked to primeval chaos through their birth in the flesh of the slain giant Ymir, they had a subtle understanding of primal forces—an understanding that gave them power to stem the tide of chaos.

With his dwarf-wrought hammer, Thor kept the frost giants at bay, although they were ceaselessly restive. Two other threats to the cosmos, a pair of serpents, reposed in menacing quiescence, one at the base of the created universe, the other in the depths of the world-girdling ocean. But a final monstrous threat—a beast called the Fenris wolf—arose soon after the world was shaped, and the gods were certain that it would be their undoing.

Once again it was Loki who brought sorrow on Asgard: The Fenris wolf was his offspring, sired by him on a giantess. At first, the gods were happy to let the wolf roam freely through Asgard's endless corridors, for it was endowed with speech, and it was, after all, their own kin. But the wolf's eyes shone with cunning and ferocity beyond the common run of beasts, and soon only Tyr, bravest of the gods, dared to toss joints of meat into its slavering jaws. Day by day the monster grew, until it was as tall as a horse and as massive as an ox, and its cries of blood lust resounded through Asgard. The three Norns—dour sisters who among them knew every event of past, present and future—declared that the wolf, unchecked, would surely destroy the gods and all they had created.

In hushed and fearful council, the gods resolved to shackle the monster. But their stoutest chains merely enraged the wolf when it felt the cold touch of metal through its fur, and when the shackles were made fast, the beast thrashed until the iron links parted like putty. The gods knew then that the wolf was a force of cosmic upheaval and that a restraint far stronger than ordinary metal would be needed. Despairing, they sent a messenger to the middle earth. Only the dwarfs could devise a bond incorporating powers as elemental and intractable as the wolf's.

Arriving in the dwarfs' subterranean realm, the messenger from Asgard conveyed the gods' entreaty. Eager as always for acclaim in the upper world, the dwarfs promised to do their utmost. They hud-

dled in conference, then approached the red maw of a furnace. Suddenly the messenger shut his eyes and staggered back in pain. The dull glow of the furnace had flared to a searing blue-white, and waves of heat had pummeled him. A moment later, though, a dwarf tapped his elbow, and the messenger risked a glance.

Draped over the dwarf's neck and around his forearm was a cord as lank and slender as a silken ribbon. "It is called Gleipnir," said the dwarf, "and it has strength the eye cannot discern, enough to shackle the wolf until the end of the world. It is made of all the secret and impalpable things of the earth: the footfall of a cat, the beard of a woman, the sinews of a bear, the roots of a rock, the breath of a fish and the spittle of a bird. And its powers are as rare and subtle as its makings." Overcome with wonder and bafflement, the messenger took the cord and hastened back to the high fortress of the gods.

They were skeptical of the fetter's strength, and when the messenger repeated the dwarf's words, they grew more dubious still. But the wolf snuffled and scratched at the great hall's doors, and the gods could waste no more time in debate. They ventured out into the corridor, Gleipnir in hand. The wolf eyed them hungrily as they approached, but its lids narrowed when they suggested that it try its strength against the cord.

In a bellow that terrified the bold and warlike gods, the wolf voiced its suspicions. If the fetter was as insubstantial as it seemed, the wolf would gain no glory by

The life-giving sun of mortals and gods brought death to dwarfs. Tricked
by a god one night, the prideful Alvíss remembered the curse of his race
too late and was turned to stone by the first light of dawn.

snapping it, and did not care to try. And if it had been strengthened with magic, the wolf would not let the cord bind its limbs.

The gods countered with wiles, saying that if the wolf could not snap so slender a bond, they would fear it no longer, and would release it. The wolf considered, then consented – providing that one god place a hand between its fangs while the fetter was in place, as a sign of good faith and a security for the beast's freedom.

Brave Tyr agreed to this, and the long, supple cord was twined again and again around the beast's limbs until the wolf seemed a vast insect caught in a silken web. Then Gleipnir was cinched tight, and with a snarl the wolf thrashed against the bonds. The gods drew back in fear – all except Tyr, who knelt at the wolf's snout, his wrist clamped between the cold fangs.

But the fetter showed its strength. Although the wolf raged and struggled, the cord did not snap; it cinched tighter and tighter until the wolf gasped for breath and could hardly even quiver within the shimmering trammels. At last, knowing it was defeated, it made Tyr pay the price, biting savagely through muscle and bone while the god shrieked, then staggered back, the stump of his wrist spouting blood.

The Fenris wolf was bound. The gods hefted the beast, inert but for a hideous yowling and a stream of slaver that ran from its chops, and carried it to a great boulder perched at the dizzy edge of Asgard. They looped the remaining length of Gleipnir around the rock and knotted it tight. Then they gagged the wolf with a sword, jamming the pommel into the lower jaw and spiking the beast's palate with the point. Finally, with words of praise for the bravery of Tyr and the cunning of the dwarfs, they buried the boulder deep in the earth of Midgard and left the wolf to languish until the end of time.

The magical fetter was a material embodiment of dwarfs' profound and subtle knowledge, but their wisdom took other forms, less tangible yet equally dazzling. It is no surprise that dwarfs, capable of breathing life into cold metal, were masters of incantations and the runic alphabet used in the ancient Norse world for mystic inscriptions. But in those days, the terms of magic were not the only words that manifested power and knowledge. The world was new, and the names for much that it contained had yet to be discovered. Simply to call an object by its rightful name was to display wisdom. And dwarfs had such wisdom in abundance.

For a dwarf named Alvíss, meaning "all-knowing," wise speech was a gift that brought triumph and misfortune. Alvíss, like other dwarfs, was prey to lust, and he was also typical in his pride and ambition: When he sought a mate, only a goddess would do. Through subterfuges too devious to have been recorded, he eventually won the right to Thor's daughter. One evening after daylight had faded and it was safe for a dwarf to roam abroad, he arrived at the gates of Asgard to claim his bride. But Thor blocked his way, saying he knew nothing of the match.

Standing in the gateway with his arms clasped, Thor towered over his dwarfish supplicant – a poor match for his daughter,

The Eddas recorded many other tales of dwarfs undone by arrogance, lust or brutality. Wisdom gave these ancestral dwarfs powers that compensated for their physical frailty, but it did not ennoble them. Their links to death, rot and the soil were spiritual as well as physical. They were the product of a primeval crime, and their character seemed irredeemably stained by their heritage.

In some ways dwarfs were simply creatures of their age. The gods were cunning and brutal, and only through equal measures of deceit and cruelty could dwarfs hope to gain the advantage—or even to hold their own. And the first mortals were no better. Their dealings with the proud and potent dwarfs bared the harshest elements in the characters of both.

Such was the case in the Eddic tale of Völund, a dwarf smith who was ill-used, and who took a barbaric revenge. With the passage of time, the story has blurred and lost detail. But the play of passions remains clear enough.

Völund was a hermit, a forest-dwelling smith whose fame had spread through all the planes of creation. Tales of his weapons of bright steel, his caldrons and goblets of inlaid silver and, most of all, his rich and intricate work in gold aroused the grasping nature of a mortal Queen. She ordered her weak-willed husband to take Völund prisoner, so that she alone could enjoy the fruits of his talent. But when the shackled dwarf was dragged before her, she saw the hatred in his eyes and took another step to secure her prize: She or-

to be sure. The dwarf was squat and lumpy as a potato, pale as a corpse from living without sun. His thick face was twisted with helpless fury, but Thor, feeling sportive, decided to toy with the dwarf. "You will have my daughter's love, wise guest, if you can answer questions about all the things of heaven and earth."

Throughout the night the god challenged the dwarf to name the features of the cosmos, and Alvíss responded with terms so obscure but so apt that Thor was astonished despite himself. But, delighting in his own eloquence, the dwarf had forgotten his weakness. The eastern sky was a wash of gray when the dwarf finished his discourse, and as Thor praised him, a ray of sunshine knifed across the cloud-tops that spread beneath Asgard.

"The day is upon you, O dwarf," said Thor, laughing at the success of his ruse. As the golden sunlight bathed his pale form, Alvíss shrieked—but his cry was cut short as his throat closed and his limbs stiffened into stone.

dered the soldiers to cut the sinews of his legs, hobbling him. Then she confined the dwarf on an island in a lake, with food, fuel and a forge, to ply his trade for her.

But the first treasures that Völund sent to the castle—bowls of bone bound with silver and brooches set with nubs of ivory—embodied a ghoulish revenge. For the two young sons of the royal couple had ventured to Völund's island to see the marvels of his smithy. As the lads gaped, the crippled dwarf, still quick with a dagger, had crept up behind them and severed their heads. He scooped out their brains and pried out their teeth, and so it was that the King and Queen unwittingly drank from their sons' brainpans and adorned themselves with their sons' white teeth.

But that did not still Völund's vengeful fury. When the lads' unsuspecting sister rowed out to the island to ask the smith to repair a ring, he offered her drugged ale. Hot with lust and vengeance, he ravished her inert body as she slept. Then he left her, a misbegotten child quickening in her womb. He took from a hiding place wings made of gold beaten to airy thinness—the product of many nights' secret work over a banked fire—and fitted them to his humped shoulders. With helpless legs dangling, he rose from his island prison.

Alighting in the royal hall, he laughingly told the King and Queen of their children's fates. He left them broken and sorrowing, his revenge complete, and rose into the night sky with heavy wingbeats, the gold of his wings flashing in the light of the watch fires, on his way back to his lonely forge in the forest.

Barbarity bred barbarity; some might say that Völund could not be blamed. But scattered through the lore of the Norse dwarfs are episodes of unprovoked cruelty, bespeaking a strain of true malignancy in the character of dwarfs. Even the grandest deeds of these ancestral dwarfs often were steeped in blood and treachery.

According to the Eddas, mortal poets owed their inspiration to the Mead of Poetry, a liquor distilled by dwarfs at the beginning of time. The dwarfs who compounded it earned fame and the gratitude of posterity. But the details of the act are those of a fearful crime.

The Eddic tale tells of a band of dwarfs who invited Kvasir, the wise adviser of the gods, to feast with them in their subterranean lair. After the meat and ale, two of the dwarfs motioned the comely god into a side chamber. They wanted, they said, to take counsel with him in private. But when the god drew close to hear their queries, they pulled daggers from their tunics and plunged them again and again into their guest. Dropping their weapons, they held kettles to the spouting wounds, clinging to the stricken Kvasir as he lurched about the cavern.

It was a ghoulish act, and premeditated. The dwarfs sought Kvasir's blood because it was tinctured with wisdom. When the murderers emerged from the chamber, holding high their pots of gore, their comrades cheered. They ladled honey into the blood, then sealed it into three vessels. With time, it became a mead so heady with inspiration that it brought the gift of verse to any whose lips it touched.

One creation of the dwarf smith Völund was a pair of golden wings to free him from an island prison. But he also turned his skills to purposes of revenge, crafting jewelry and goblets from human teeth and skulls. . . .

The sublime gift of mortal inspiration had a sinister source: Dwarfs murdered a counselor of the gods and brewed his blood with honey to make the Mead of Poetry.

The dwarfs did not profit from their grisly enterprise. The mead's guardians soon were forced to surrender it to a giant as the price of their lives when, in another spasm of brutality, they murdered the giant's parents. And in the end, by a tortuous route, the distilled wisdom of their slain counselor returned to the gods. There it remained ever after, according to the Eddas, and the gods dispensed it as they pleased to mortal poets.

That their crime should have blessed future generations with poetry is in keeping with the paradoxical nature of the ancestral dwarfs. They emerge from the terse, fragmented Eddic accounts as a mass of contradictions: They coupled prowess at crafts with physical infirmity, wisdom with pride and folly. And their legacy to the mortals and diminished dwarfs who inherited the earth reflects their complex role in the elemental world of the gods.

Many of their skills lived on. Later dwarfs possessed their ancestors' gift for metalworking, although they never raised it to the same supernaturally fine art. Mortal wizards chanted spells once muttered by dwarfs; mortal bards profited by the runic alphabet. The truest embodiments of dwarfs' ancient powers, the wondrous objects of their forges, also survived their makers' decline, lingering into the next ages in lost treasure hoards and as the heirlooms of families of long and distinguished lineage. Often endowed with supernatural virtues, the treasures were reminders of forgotten mysteries.

These fabulous trinkets and weapons also preserved the dark side of their makers' character. Curses, inextricably entwined with the objects' magical vitality, made them as perilous as they were beautiful. Tales tell of mortal clans doomed to strife and suffering because of a dwarf-cursed treasure they harbored. Yet it is testimony to the powers of the dwarfs who dwelled at the dawn of the earth that their curses, the scourge of generations, often resulted from nothing more than pique.

Pique alone drove a dwarf named Andvari to invest a gold ring with fateful powers. The ring, like the charmed armband made by the brothers Brokk and Sindri, had the power to spawn wealth. According to a tale told in the Eddas, the gods themselves wrested the precious object from Andvari, and that injustice is what drew the dwarf's ire. Here is how it happened:

Strolling among the woods and swamps of Midgard, a trio of gods — Loki among them — stoned and killed an otter for their supper, unaware that its animal form concealed the shape-shifting son of an elfin magician. The magician demanded blood money — enough gold to fill and cover the otter's skin completely. Only Andvari possessed wealth enough, and Loki hastened to the realm of the dwarfs to win his treasure by guile or force.

When he arrived in Andvari's grotto, the dwarf was nowhere to be seen. But in a pool of water, a silvery pike whipped and darted. Guessing the dwarf's ruse, Loki plunged his hands into the water and closed them around the fish. At that instant the pike vanished. In its place a hideous dwarf splashed and spluttered.

Holding Andvari tight as he hauled him from the water, Loki demanded his treasure, and when the god released him, the dwarf obliged with apronloads of gold. But as he tossed a final few trinkets into Loki's sack, the dwarf kept one fist clenched. Loki pried back the stubby fingers, and there lay a plain gold ring — no prize, but acceptable for blood payment.

He tossed it into his sack while the dwarf pleaded and protested. Finally, hopeless of retaining the ring, Andvari cursed it: "My wealth will prove a false delight; the ring will destroy all who possess it."

Typical of his race, Andvari was potent even in his degradation. With the curse, the dwarf loosed a tide of tragedy that washed over every guardian of the hoard, beginning with the magician who took it as blood money for his son. Another son, coveting the gold, slew the magician to possess it. Then a third son became the curse's instrument: Inflamed by greed, he enlisted the mortal hero Sigurd to murder his brother. But when the deed was done, Sigurd feared treachery, and he killed the third brother, the last of the magician's sons, and himself took possession of the hoard. His life, too, was blighted and his death hastened by the fateful ring.

As centuries passed, Andvari's treasure lost none of its evil luster, but the race that had spawned it fell into decline. The young breed of mortals grew in number and power, and dwarfs gradually retreated to distant kingdoms or sought secluded niches within the mortal peasants' world of farms and fields. Their character changed with their station; as their traffic with gods ended, dwarfs, no longer cosmic actors, grew mild-mannered, even humble.

But the legacy of the first age remained potent. They preserved the shadowy arts of their ancestors, practicing them far from the sight of their human neighbors. Even in the humblest of later dwarfs, wary mortals sensed a trace of the old powers, awesome and unspeakable, passed down the bloodlines from lordly forebears

A Blade Charged with Vengeance

The earliest dwarfs used their talents to supply mortal heroes with weapons of rare potency, but the magic that gave these arms their wondrous traits often was touched with evil, as the tale of Svafrlami shows:

Svafrlami was the warlike ruler of a land of forests, bogs and lakes in what was later Russia. The land was as wild as its master; terrors lurked in the trackless woods beyond the palisade enclosing the King's stronghold, and few members of the court cared to stray from the compound. But Svafrlami himself was afraid of nothing. For diversion, he often would shoulder his bow and ride out to hunt deer and boar.

Late one afternoon, after a day of solitary hunting, he spied a stag in the slanting light of a distant clearing. He gave chase, but he could not gain on the animal. The parklike stand of birches he galloped through gave way to a dense forest, whose floor was a tumble of boulders. The darkness thickened among those birches, and Svafrlami lost sight of the deer. He glimpsed a new quarry, however: At the base of a boulder, two pallid faces watched the mortal King, dark eyes gazing from corpse gray skin. They were dwarfs, Durin and Dvalin by name, and they crouched low in the gathering shadows, rigidly wary, while the King dismounted and sauntered past, pretending not to see them.

Suddenly Svafrlami whirled, sweeping his sword from its scabbard. He brought the blade down with all his might, so that it bit

deep into the stony soil behind the dwarfs, cutting off their route of retreat into the boulder that served as their home. Trapped, the dwarfs flung themselves to the ground, grinding their faces into the earth and uttering muffled cries of terror.

Svafrlami grabbed the pair and hauled them to their feet to hear his demand. He would spare their lives, he said, if they forged him a sword that would surpass any in mortal possession. It should never dull, it should cut through iron and stone as if through cloth, and it should bring its owner victory in every battle. The dwarfs regarded him with fear and hostility, but they were helpless to refuse: Svafrlami was capable of holding them until daylight came, and daylight was the thing they dreaded above all

else. When they had given their word, the man permitted them free passage into the rock. In an instant, they were gone.

As the night insects droned and the moonlight silhouetted the trees, Svafrlami dozed, pillowing his head against the dwarfs' boulder. He awoke at intervals to see showers of sparks cascade from the rock and hear the screech and clang of the dwarfs at work. Just before the dawn, he awoke again: The dwarfs had reappeared, and they carried a broadsword, massive and fine.

Its scabbard was golden, and on it, in high relief, were depicted the deeds of the

old gods. Guard, grip and pommel were of gold as well, winking with jewels. Svafrlami grasped the weapon, and when he drew the blade, he saw that the steel was bright and flawless. As he turned it, the metal magically flashed sun-dazzle into his eyes, although the sun still lay below the horizon.

He turned his gaze to the sword's creators and met a look of malevolent amusement.

"It is all you asked, and more," said Dvalin. "Its name is Tyrfing, and to the qualities you demanded, it adds these: Once drawn, it cannot be sheathed unless it is warm with human blood. It will figure in three atrocious crimes. You yourself will die by its keen edge."

His face darkening with rage, Svafrlami swung at the dwarfs, but they skipped aside, and Tyrfing cleft the rock behind them. They fled, leaving Svafrlami alone to regard his perilous prize.

In fact, he could not sheathe the weapon for many days—until the charmed sword had proved its worth on the flesh of his enemies in battle. And as the dwarfs intended, Svafrlami himself felt Tyrfing's cold bite some months later. Here is what happened:

A raider from another country harried the fringes of his realm and, as was the custom, Svafrlami sallied forth to meet him in single combat. On a windy plain the two men fought, until Svafrlami's sword glanced from the iron-banded shield of his opponent and sank into the earth. The King struggled to pull it free, but before he could succeed, his enemy severed Svafrlami's hand at the wrist with a swift stroke. Then he dragged Tyrfing from the earth and hewed Svafrlami to the ground. Now the sword was his, and he used it to good effect. He led his warriors across Svafrlami's domain, slew the defenders by the hundreds and sold Svafrlami's kin into slavery.

But the raider and his descendants profited no more from the radiant sword than had Svafrlami. As Tyrfing, perversely prized, was passed down the generations, brother wielded it against brother and son against father. The kin slayings in which it figured were three in all; then, having shed its appointed quantity of blood, the dwarf sword vanished from the chronicles.

Chapter Two

The Diminutive Nobility

When Europe was still sundered into a mosaic of duchies, counties and baronies, bound in shifting patterns of alliance and feudal loyalty, knights and lords often were called upon to lend their fighting skills to the cause of a fellow nobleman. But few such requests were like the one received by Wilhelm von Scherfenberg, who ruled a district of grass-clad uplands and rich, well-watered valleys in the Tyrol. Here is that tale:

Weary of his round of peacetime duties, of hours spent hearing the reports of his stewards and judging peasants' disputes, Scherfenberg lounged late one afternoon on a stone sill high in the walls of his castle, daydreaming of battle and gazing out at the flower-spangled meadows that spread beneath the fortifications. A stir and a shimmer caught his eye, and he watched in astonishment as a procession approached. Flanked by attendants and followed by a pair of elegant grey-hounds, a crowned King made his way up the slopes. He rode beneath a canopy of brocaded silk, and he and his mount both were so heavily encrusted with gold and gems that they seemed united as a single glittering statue.

Scherfenberg's wonder quickly gave way to annoyance: It was an affront for a strange king to flaunt his magnificence in this unannounced way. The lord seized sword and shield and hurried to the castle gate to demand an explanation.

Yet he was awed once again when he crossed the moat and waded through the tall grass toward the noble travelers. They flashed in and out of view behind shrubs no higher than Scherfenberg's waist, and the silken canopy was dusted pale yellow with pollen from the

tallest wild flowers. Suddenly Scherfenberg realized that the splendid procession was miniature: The King and all of his retainers were dwarfs.

Warily, he approached the troop. When the kingly rider drew rein, Scherfenberg gazed under the canopy, where gems gleamed and flashed. He saw a face that was fine of feature but seamed with incalculable age. Dark eyes, wise and appraising, regarded him steadily. Then the dwarf greeted him by name and in a high and ancient voice asked Scherfenberg to hear his appeal. He declared that he was no freak, but a lord like the mortal. Although his domain lay underground, beneath savage mountains, he governed it by the same lights of justice and wisdom as the best of mortal kings.

Now, however, war had flared up between him and a neighboring dwarf lord, and he needed help. The Dwarf King had heard much of Scherfenberg's courage in battle and skill at arms, and he sought from him a pledge of aid.

The mortal lord drew himself up, ready to assent, for no man of mettle could spurn so graceful a request, but the dwarf continued. "If you agree to do battle for me, I will gird you with a belt that gives its wearer the strength of twenty, so that even if my foe sends forth a giant, you will not falter. And as a sign of my good faith and magical powers, I now present you with a ring that ensures its wearer's wealth." Scherfenberg bowed deeply. When he again raised his eyes, one atten-dant held out a simple ring of gold. "Tell no one of your pledge, not even your wife," said the Dwarf King as the mortal took the ring, "but return to this mountain meadow tomorrow, armed and mounted, for my need is dire." Then he swung about, his attendants raised the silken canopy above him, and the little group wended its way through the flowers and dancing butterflies to the shoulder of the mountainside, where it was lost to view.

Yet that night Scherfenberg's actions betrayed his plans. He directed his squire to polish his breastplate and scour the rust from his sword; he ordered the stable-hands to prepare his war horse for the morning; and he sent for the priest to hear his confession. As he sat at the board to sup, he was silent and thoughtful, anticipating the next day's struggle.

His wife noticed all. She sent courtiers to bully the priest into revealing her husband's confession. When she learned of his intention to battle a dwarf lord, she feared that he would face an onslaught of magic against which his strength and valor would be helpless. She pleaded with him — and awakened his own buried fears. In the end he agreed to break his pledge.

But he was shamefaced, and for many months he did not stray from his castle to ride through his domain. When at last he clattered over the moat and out into his lands, winter had dusted the meadows and pines with an early snow. He wandered aimlessly for hours, confused at heart, alone with his bleak thoughts in the hush that held the land. Then Scherfenberg heard the patter of tiny hoofs. The Dwarf King drew even with him.

The mortal turned, half fearful and half defiant, to confront the seamed and weary face in its setting of gems and woven gold. Although the dwarf rose no higher than Scherfenberg's stirrup and had to tip his crowned head far back to meet the human's eyes, his face was hardened with contempt. "Wilhelm," he said, "you have deceived and betrayed me. I would take back the magical ring I gave you, but you could defeat me in a contest of strength. Still, I am your better at magic, and I now doom you never again to see victory in battle. You deserve no better fate." Having delivered these harsh words, he turned and spurred his horse up the mountainside, making for a rockfall far up the slope. There the brightness winked out: The dwarf had vanished.

Thereafter, Scherfenberg lurched from defeat to ignominious defeat, although his enemies never succeeded in seizing his castle and lands, for his property was protected by the Dwarf King's ring. Finally, he fell in battle, pierced by an enemy spear. Death alone could end his long humiliation and release him from the invisible coils of the dwarf's curse.

To engender and protect wealth with a little circle of gold, to doom a man to perennial defeat—these were mighty powers in mortals' eyes. Yet for all his potency, the Dwarf King represented a diminished race. As a people, dwarfs had been eclipsed by the earth's new, human children. Most dwarfs had abandoned the expansive ways of times when they consorted with gods. Gone was their ability—

or perhaps it was their will—to join in cosmic struggles against the forces of chaos, as they had done in ages past. They now dwelled close to the land, turning their magical artifice to humble crafts and, for the most part, leading lives as anonymous and full of toil as the mortal peasants whose ways they mirrored.

But a few of them sparkled with some of the old glory and even surpassed their rock-dwelling ancestors in grace and splendor. These were the dwarf kings, among them Scherfenberg's supplicant, who ruled treasure-filled domains underground—realms brighter and more fragile than those of their mortal counterparts.

The jewel-like lands of the dwarfs had no chroniclers of their own, and they were hidden from the mass of humankind. But adventurers sometimes broached them—for the most part high-born knights thirsty for new fields on which to prove their valor. Thus, glimpses of dwarf realms are to be found in the records of mortal heroes and their deeds.

Those tales, however, were intended as much to entertain and instruct their audiences as to reveal the truth; they were therefore given to exaggeration and moralizing, and the picture of dwarf domains is hazy with wishful thinking.

Still, certain patterns emerge from the tales. Often, for example, the quests and triumphs of human heroes hinged on the magical powers of dwarfs. In much the same way that ancestral dwarfs rendered aid to the gods in battles against the forces that menaced creation, the dwarfs' royal descendants supplied mortals with charms and weapons of uncommon virtue. So it was with the great dragonslayer Siegfried: The gaining of dwarf-forged weaponry completed his preparation for a life of unmatched heroism.

Siegfried's formal anointing as a knight took place in the Low Countries at the court of his father, where the young Prince knelt to receive broadsword and armor while the assembled nobles cheered and drained beakers of wine. But weapons made by mortals were not equal to the destiny of that young man.

With his untried blade swinging beside his stirrup, Siegfried rode out into the forest and heath of the young earth to seek adventure. In a land unnamed in the chronicles, far up the wooded path he was following, two dwarfs clad in the patterned garb of heralds slipped from the dark firs and hailed him. As he approached, they fell to their knees and begged his aid.

They were the envoys of a dwarf people called the Nibelungs, whose King had died. In the cavern that was the realm of the Nibelungs, the King's two sons were bickering over their father's treasure, so great in quantity that it would have filled one hundred oxcarts. To end the strife, their subjects sought an impartial judge, and they promised Siegfried a handsome reward for his services.

After the young knight assented, the envoys led him off the path through the moss-floored forest to a looming cliff. There, at a signal, a stream of dwarfs poured from a cleft in the rock, emptying baskets of gold and gems onto the stony ground. On and on they came, mounding up the yield of untold centuries of delv-

ing and smithwork, until they had built a treasure dune almost too bright to look upon. It spread around the ankles of Siegfried where he stood and washed up against the face of the cliff like a tide. When at last the column of bearers slackened and stopped, a party of dwarf notables, pale and blinking, slipped from the cleft and stationed themselves close by as Siegfried made his division.

The task took all day. Siegfried counted and calculated and appraised, holding each winking gem to the light to judge its worth, all under the watchful eyes of the two silk-clad Dwarf Princes. As the hours passed, he separated the treasure into two huge, scintillating piles. Then, tossing the last trinket onto one of the piles to make them exactly the same, he turned to the Princes and demanded his reward.

Grudgingly, they ordered a party of servants into the cave. When the servants returned, they carried on their shoulders a sword so supple that, with the rhythm of their tread, it rippled like wind-blown grain. But its edge was keen far beyond mortal craft. A butterfly that blundered against the blade as Siegfried took the sword in hand was divided neatly in two and fluttered piecewise to the ground. The sword's name, the Dwarf Princes told the mortal, was Balmung.

The sword first proved its worth on the flesh of the Nibelungs themselves. A rumor took hold among the watching dwarfs that Siegfried had pocketed some of the treasure, and the murmur swelled into a clamor for the hero's blood. The avaricious Princes joined in the cry, and soon a group of dwarf champions, armored like beetles in dusky iron, strode from the cave to battle the mortal. They surrounded Siegfried and slashed at him with vicious strokes, but their collective strength was not the equal of Balmung.

Siegfried scythed down any warrior who came within reach. Then the dwarfs, seeing how things were going, resorted to powerful spells to even the odds. A thick mist descended on the field of battle, concealing the dwarf champions as they lunged at the mortal. Still, he slew each shadowy figure that made such an attempt. Next, the dwarfs summoned a great thunderstorm. Siegfried was flung off balance by gusts of wind, blinded by strokes of lightning, and deafened by the crashes of thunder that followed. Yet he withstood each assault of the storm and continued to dispatch the dwarf warriors one after another — all but the last, who swirled a dark cape around his shoulders and dissolved into nothingness just as the hero was about to cut him down.

Invisible, the dwarf champion stung Siegfried with sword strokes that fell from every direction. Only when the hero, flailing wildly at emptiness, felt his blade bite into invisible armor and flesh did the dwarf warrior reappear, severely wounded and begging for mercy. He surrendered to the hero the cloak of invisibility and agreed to serve him as keeper of the Nibelungs' treasure which now belonged to Siegfried as the spoils of battle. The hero put to death the faithless Princes; then he rode on with the dwarf-wrought sword and cape, well prepared for his high calling.

Such tales made it clear that dwarfs had lost none of their ancient gifts of artifice. Moreover, the perfidy of the Nibelung Princes and Siegfried's response to it echoed the patterns of earlier times, when cunning and treacherous dwarfs were pitted against the ruthless power of the gods. In that respect, however, the tale was unusual. Seldom were interactions between dwarfs and mortal heroes touched with the harshness of Siegfried's encounter with the Nibelung Princes.

The world had grown more ordered since the era when dwarfs trafficked with gods. In those days, the existence of mortals was coarse and brutal. A world of enemies lurked beyond the glow of the watch fires, and ferocity, untempered by any virtue other than loyalty to kinsmen and chieftain, was the quality most prized in a warrior. But with the passing centuries, the mortal realm had expanded from scattered wilderness camps of herdsmen and marauders to a domesticated landscape of pasture, plowland and village. Skeins of loyalty and interdependence had drawn mortals together into ever larger communities: manors, feudal domains and monarchies. And faith had unified the population into the largest of all communities, the Church.

Naked conflicts in the style of earlier days threatened this elaborate structure of order. Enmities now had to be contained and channeled, and new codes of conduct arose to check the excesses of fighting men. A warrior now was known as a knight, and he faced demands unknown to combatants of old. Valor was no less prized than it had been, but to courage a knight was expected to add honor, mercy toward the vanquished foe, comeliness of dress and manner, and perfect courtesy toward women.

Most knights fell far short of the ideal. The common folk, living in the shadow of the local baron's crude tower and bullied by the coarse fighting men who provided their protection, saw little chivalry near at hand. But they heard it celebrated in tales sung by wandering troubadours—accounts of great deeds and high character. Nor did these songs honor only mortals: Of those who met the standards of the chivalric ideal, said the troubadours, many were kingly dwarfs.

When singers described the court of King Arthur, for example, they liked to tell not just of radiant knights and ladies but of genteel dwarf kings. Such a one was Bilis, who arrived on a summer's day when the high towers of Camelot flew bright banners in honor of the wedding of Sir Erec, a knight of the Round Table. Bilis reigned over a land known as Antipodes—a name reflecting popular belief that it lay on the far side of the world. He had journeyed across the waters to Britain not because of ties of kinship or homage but simply out of esteem for the young and virtuous knight.

Other lords made splendid display on the occasion, and their bright tents and pavilions dotted the sunny meadows around Camelot. One lord arrived at the head of a procession of one hundred knights, all encased in silvery armor, with pennants streaming from their upraised lances like a flock of bright birds. Another came with a dazzling retinue of five hundred courtiers and ladies. In the train of yet another lord, every retainer bore on a gloved fist either a falcon or a sparrow hawk, a goshawk or an eagle, to divert the company with the sport of falconry.

When Bilis and two of his subject Kings rode up from the sea on mounts no bigger than greyhounds, they blended easily with this company. Their dress was resplendent, and they bore gifts of gems and finely worked gold. Bilis and his companions held firm and knightly converse with the other lords and delighted the ladies of the court with witty flattery. The chroniclers of Arthur's court summed them up as "very perfect gentlemen."

Knightly graces were not a matter of comportment alone; in the perfect chevalier, grace of manner reflected underlying virtue. This was no less true of the high-born dwarfs. Poets and chroniclers spoke of dwarf kings or even entire dwarf peoples whose righteousness put sinful mortals to shame. One Welsh scholar described a tribe of dwarfs whose merit, he declared, was seen not just in manner and deeds but in their very features. The source of his information was a priest named Elidor, who had met the dwarfs years before, in his boyhood.

He had been a restless lad, and one day he fled the scolding of his tutor and hid in a cave in a steep riverbank. For two days he sat under the overhang, hungry and cold, and watched the current slide past his feet.

Beyond the entrance to a cave in Wales lay a miniature kingdom, hidden from mortal view until the day two friendly dwarfs guided a boy named Elidor to its splendors.

On the third day two small figures, distinguished in mien, entered the cave.

They spoke to the forlorn boy of a land where games and laughter never ceased, and he did not hesitate when they clasped his hands and led him out of the cave, along the bank and into a deeper, darker cleft. They guided him down a long passageway that smelled of damp earth, then out into a cavernous region of twilight. Neither sun nor moon brightened its sky. The light was leaden, but their miniature villages—each set beneath a dome—gave off a lamplike glow.

From these villages, the inhabitants poured forth to gaze at the mortal boy. Their faces were at once curious and welcoming, and the lad instantly sensed that this was a wise and untroubled society. Moreover, every aspect of the underground kingdom seemed touched by beauty. The villages were graced by splendid architecture. The landscape beguiled the eye with its soft curves and lambent play of light. Bright birds crisscrossed the cavern vault. And many among the elegant dwarf company wore robes of white linen.

Elidor was lodged in the palace of the King of the country, and he soon found playmates in the children of the royal family and the courtiers. No bigger than fairies and sportive as swallows, they danced and darted and tossed golden balls as the mortal boy clumsily tried to join in their play. But sometimes they gathered around him on the glossy marble floor and chattered of their elders' love of the truth and scorn for mortal faithlessness. They asked him about the world of men and women, and grew wide-eyed with horror when Elidor told them of the human diet of flesh, fish and fowl. In their land, milk and saffron were the staples.

When, as a grown man, Elidor recalled his sojourn in the dwarf kingdom, he wept to think that he had proved unworthy of his hosts. It happened like this:

One day he pined for home, and the guides who had led him from the cave

Dishonoring the mortal race by his thieving, the boy Elidor fled from
the dwarf world with a golden prize—but he did not keep it for long.

offered to conduct him back to visit his family. His mother wept to see him alive, but when he told her of the loveliness of the dwarfs' realm, she became thoughtful. She said that he could return to their land but that he must visit her again and bring back one of his dwarf playmates' golden balls. Such a quantity of gold could buy much comfort and cheer in the mortal world. At his mother's words, Elidor felt an answering thrill of greed, and he promised to do as she asked.

He returned to the dank cave, where his guides awaited him. This time, though, his stay in the dwarf kingdom was brief. At play with a tiny Prince, the boy snatched up a golden ball and fled while the dwarf child gazed after him in astonishment, then fell to the floor, sobbing. Two palace servants chased the lad as he sped through the gentle woodlands toward the passage, and their footsteps were a pursuing staccato as he blundered through the chilly shadows. At the far end, he burst into the sunlight, clutching the ball to his chest, climbed the bank and set off across the fields to his mother's cottage. On the doorstep, he stumbled, and the golden ball thudded into the dust. The dwarfs, still following close behind, darted around him, and one of them caught up the ball in his birdlike hands. They shot him glances laden with contempt, then slipped silently back into the tall grass of the field and were gone.

Elidor watched, already consumed with remorse. During the weeks that followed, he returned to the riverbank every day to search for the muddy cleft, but the passage to the dwarf land had closed forever.

The kings and warriors of such comely tribes of dwarfs were said to live by the same demanding code as mortal knights. Yet likeness did not always beget harmony. Knights' personal quests for honor and glory inevitably led to conflict with other knights — and so it was with the dwarf nobility. Tales of courtesies and peaceable visits exchanged by mortal knights and noble dwarfs abound, but warlike encounters were more common. And the chronicles of those conflicts showed that dwarfs possessed the prowess of the best of their mortal opponents.

Single combat between a hero and a dwarf was the most common kind of clash; mortal heroes constantly sought individual demonstrations of their courage, and dwarfs, too, relished such tests of valor. But a Tyrolean tale, well known among both the German- and the Italian-speaking peasants of the district, told of a Dwarf King who struggled with his mortal neighbors on a grander scale. At issue was the highest object of a valiant knight's striving: the love of a lady.

Laurin, King of the Dwarfs, was an unlikely combatant. He was used to displaying his wisdom and virtue in the arts of peace: just rule and the pursuit of beauty. His domain enclosed a mountain range now known as the Catinaccio — Italian for "jagged chain." The name is apt; the mountains rake the sky in spikes of dolomite, utterly bare of vegetation. But during Laurin's reign, the spires, magically fertile, bore an aerial garden. A thick cloak of rosebushes mantled each pinnacle, setting the heights aglow with blossoms of pink, yellow, salmon and richest crimson. On warm summer nights, peasants dwelling in the valleys far below looked up from their chores, drank in the perfume that wafted from the lofty garden and praised its good King Laurin.

Laurin girded his realm not with a wall, a moat or other fortifications, but with a single silken thread, strung from trunk to trunk through the forests that spread at the base of the crags. And he ruled his subjects with corresponding mildness. The spires were hollow, and in their tall, echoing interiors, radiant with the light of torches reflected and intensified by the gold and gems that encrusted the walls of the caverns, Laurin's subjects danced and feasted under the benevolent gaze of their King, always to the gentle tinkle of harps and the piping of flutes. The caverns were alive with the trilling of songbirds in gilded cages and the high, gay chatter of the dwarfs themselves.

There was no strife in Laurin's domain, and very little toil—only the quiet labor of craftsmen weaving silk and soft wool into tapestries or fashioning treasures of gems and precious metals, and the tranquil work of the herdsmen who ventured out of the hollow mountains into the forest-girded meadows to tend their flocks of goats and milch cows.

His subjects lived in cheer and harmony, and Laurin one day resolved to complete his own happiness by seeking a wife. His station barred him from wedding any of the common maidens of his realm, and his fellow dwarf monarchs, reigning in similar splendor beneath surrounding

peaks, had no marriageable daughters. But the dwarf herdsmen sometimes encountered mortal woodsmen and guides, and from such meetings news had reached Laurin of a mortal Princess of surpassing wit and beauty. Her name was Similde, and she dwelled far to the south, in a kingdom of black earth, dusky vineyards and red-roofed villages.

The Dwarf King resolved to wed her, and he sent envoys to the southern kingdom. The little party, three in all, set out from the mountain fastness in a regalia of silk and gold, studded with gems that shone in the sunshine. The company led a pygmy packhorse burdened with gifts for the mortal King, and as the travelers pressed south through pine forests and along rushing streams, they sang in high, fluting voices of their master's love.

Many weeks later, two of the messengers returned, tattered and despondent, to tell their tale. The gatekeeper at the palace of the southern King was an uncouth knight named Vitege. Arms clasped above his swollen belly, he had sneered at the envoys as they stood erect and dignified at his feet, proudly reciting their master's request. He barred their way and scoffed at Laurin's presumption in thinking that a mortal princess would have him.

In the end, other guards, who were impressed by the courteous demeanor of the dwarf messengers, forced Vitege to stand aside. The ambassadors fared no better, however, in the throne room; the Princess, overhearing their suit to the King, was terrified at the prospect of wedding an otherworldly monarch and dwelling in a strange and distant land. She fell at her father's feet, weeping, and the messengers were swiftly shown out.

Gleeful at the failure of King Laurin's suit, Vitege heckled the dwarf messengers as they left the palace, and they primly rebuked him for his discourtesy. Infuriated, he chased them out into the dusty lane, snagging them and pinning all three against his chest with one thick arm. With a chortle, Vitege drew his sword and cut the throat of one dwarf, then stripped the other two of their treasures and sent them on their way with a kick and a sneer.

On hearing his messengers' account, Laurin became silent with rage, but he was not defeated. This time it was the King himself who set out on the long journey to the southern court, and he was prepared not with gifts and fine phrases of entreaty but with

Desirous of a human bride, the Dwarf King Laurin
left his mountain realm and, in the shape of a puff of
thistledown, rode the breeze long miles to the south.

a magical cloak that rendered invisible anything it enfolded. Laurin did not toil along the weary path his envoys had followed; his patience was short. Instead, he stood at the gates of his realm and intoned spells. His figure grew milky and translucent. Then it faded altogether, leaving a wisp of thistledown drifting slowly toward the ground.

Suddenly a gust of wind caught the thistledown, and in that feathery guise Laurin was wafted out of his mountainous dominion and up into the high azure sky that arched over the southern plain. He sank gently toward the spires of the palace that sheltered Similde, slipped into the shadow of a high-walled garden and landed on the grass beneath a linden tree.

Then Laurin returned to his wonted shape, at the same time spreading his cloak of invisibility so that nothing more than a puff of breeze betrayed his arrival. He gazed about the garden, and his heart contracted with love when he saw Similde, strolling nearby with a bunch of blossoms clasped in her slender hand, her tread so light that it did not even bruise the blades of grass. Repute had not exaggerated the beauty of the Princess. The Dwarf King stood for a moment in silent contemplation of the tall mortal maiden before putting his plan into action.

When Similde strayed near the linden tree, Laurin invoked the most powerful spells he knew. Similde felt her limbs grow light and tremulous, and she began to sway with the lightest breath of wind.

Then her sight darkened and she was lost in a faint. Laurin watched with satisfaction as she dwindled into a puff of thistledown. He caught the airy wisp and turned into thistledown himself. Tangled with his captive in a cottony mass, he summoned up a wind that launched them high into the air, where they gently dipped and rose together on breezes that carried them back to Laurin's kingdom.

For seven years Similde dwelled with the dwarfs, reigning by the Dwarf King's side. At first she was an unwilling Queen: She pined for her family, her sunny kingdom and the dashing knights who had courted her. But with each passing day the memory of home faded, and King Laurin, unfailingly kind and gentle, won a place in Similde's heart.

Her family, however, was desolate and had never ceased searching for her. At last a charcoal burner knocked at the palace gates, offering news of Similde in exchange for a reward. In the deep forests that cloaked the distant peaks, the man had met a dwarf who boasted of the wise and beautiful mortal Princess whom his King had taken to wife. That Princess could only be Similde.

Her brother immediately laid plans to rescue her. He summoned the palace knights and sent messengers to ask the aid of two great heroes of the day: Theodoric of Verona, a slayer of dragons, and a wise old warrior named Hildebrand.

Sun beating on armor, pennants slack in the still air, the assembled host set off across the plain to the saw-toothed line of mountains that guarded the horizon. The terrain steepened, and the men wound into the defiles in a silvery stream of armor. As the peaks rose higher and closer and hawks circled the sunlit heights far above the men, the knights began to despair of their quest. But Hildebrand, remembering from old tales that the Dwarf King's realm was as remote as it was glorious, urged them on.

Finally the peaks opened into a rolling upland of forests and meadows. A sweet scent of roses washed over the company, and the knights paused to marvel at the spectacle before them: a row of pinnacles like flaming torches, soaring skyward from the dark pines, each spire wreathed in a luminous haze of blossom.

With a cry of joy the men plunged into the forest. The scent of roses grew heavier as the knights pressed on through the pines. Soon, rosebushes glimmered in the shadowy undergrowth, all in full bloom. Then the knights came to a clearing where their way was barred by a single silken thread, aglow like a sunstruck cobweb. Beyond spread unbroken billows of roses, steepening into a flower-cloaked peak.

The warriors' thirst for battle ebbed at the sight. None wished to harm the kingdom except for Vitege, who cursed the vanity and presumption of Laurin's beautiful garden. He drew his sword, severed the thread and stormed into the rosebushes, slashing at them until his blade ran with sap.

At once there was a stir, and the knights glanced up the slope to see a diminutive horseman spurring his way down a flower-lined alley. His splendor left no doubt that he was Laurin: He wore breastplate and greaves of beaten gold, and the rest of his body was clad in golden mail so fine and supple that it might have been his own skin. He bore a shield ablaze with gems and he rode a charger as small and nimble as a fawn. When he drew up before the despoiler of his garden, jeweled larks and nightingales, cunningly sculpted into his golden helmet, fluted and trilled with magical life. King Laurin dismounted and drew his sword.

It was Vitege who struck the first blow, but his sword glanced harmlessly off Laurin's shield. Then the dwarf countered with the strength of a company of knights, plying his sword so lustily that Vitege soon lay battered and bleeding among the briers. Theodoric sallied forth to avenge his comrade in arms, but the hero fared no better. His thunderous blows rattled impotently against the armor of the dwarf, who returned strokes so cruel that they bit deep into Theodoric's armor and purpled it with blood.

Reeling with pain and exhaustion, the hero was on the point of pleading for mercy when Hildebrand, who had been watching the contest closely, declared that the dwarf's armor was magically strengthened and impenetrable. Hildebrand had noticed, as well, a subtly patterned belt knotted around the Dwarf King's waist, and he guessed it to be the source of Laurin's supernatural strength. "Rain blows on his head until he staggers," the old warrior cried to Theodoric, "then snatch his belt, and he will be in your power."

It was as Hildebrand had said. Once Theodoric had torn the belt from the dwarf's waist, King Laurin's sword strokes were harmless, and he fought with the vain fury of an angry child. Soon the dwarf lowered his weapon, despairing. He raised his visor, fell to one knee and humbly beseeched Theodoric for mercy.

So graceful were the dwarf's phrases, and so refined the countenance that looked up at the mortal knight from within the golden helmet, that Theodoric was moved to lift his foe to his feet and clasp his hands fervently. He offered to swear peace and brotherhood with the Dwarf King, and Laurin joyfully agreed. From the watching company, however, came the voice of Similde's brother, demanding news of the Princess.

The Dwarf King smiled, pleased to answer. "Queen Similde is happy, and as radiant as ever. She dwells with me in the mountain that rises before us, and I invite you all into my domain, to see for yourselves the truth of my words, and to celebrate our new brotherhood." Then Laurin mounted his charger and led the procession of mortal knights up the petal-strewn alleys of roses to a looming cliff.

A leather rope dangled from the rock, and Laurin tugged it, sounding a bell high on the face of the cliff. From a nearby cleft there issued the screeching of hinges. Laurin motioned the knights through tall iron gates, swung open by gangs of dwarfs. Beyond the gates lay a world of light, where all was laughter and revelry. On a glittering dais sat Queen Similde, smiling and animated, dwarf re-

tainers swarming about her feet. Dazzled, the mortal knights joined the throng.

That was the happy climax of relations between Laurin and the mortals. The sad events that followed are a matter of dispute. Some storytellers claim that Laurin was meditating treachery when he issued the invitation to the knights to enter the hollow mountain, that he planned to bespell them and slaughter them, but that Similde gave Theodoric charms to counter the dwarfish enchantments, enabling the

Mortal warriors, determined to return Similde to her homeland, invaded
Laurin's flowery kingdom and vanquished him by stripping off his magical belt.

mortals to prevail. Laurin's noble character makes such a tale hard to credit, however.

Another version of the woeful episode rings truer. Vitege, unreconciled to Laurin and galled by his hospitality, quarreled with some of the dwarfs during the feasting. Hearing the disturbance, the other knights suspected betrayal, and they fell on their dwarfish hosts. The battle ebbed and surged, but in the end the dwarfs were overcome and butchered. Similde, sorrowing, was led off by her brother. And Laurin was borne away in chains.

At the palace of the southern King, Vitege was Laurin's jailer, and the boorish knight added to the dwarf's humiliation by forcing him, collared and leashed, to dance atop a barrel while his captors guffawed. So broken in spirit was the fallen King that his charms had no power, and he gained his freedom only by luck. One night his guards dozed off after a bout of cards and ale. Laurin edged close to their fire and burned through his leather fetter, then fled for his mountain domain. When he crested the peaks that enclosed his realm, his heart leaped at the sight of the rose garden in the half-light of dawn — then sank at the thought that its beauty had been a beacon for the mortal invaders. Sadly, he doomed the flowers never again to show their hues by day or to shed their scent by night. Entering his lofty hall,

he found that his remaining subjects were still loyal; with time, the Dwarf King would restore his underground kingdom to its former splendor. On the high slopes, however, the petals withered and curled. The brilliant hues faded to brown, and the briers died to a dry network of roots and stems. Soon wind and decay left the spires bare and forbidding.

But the peasants who told the tale claimed that Laurin's garden had not disappeared altogether. By day and by night its glory had vanished. Yet in his curse Laurin overlooked the in-between hours of dawn and dusk, and at those moments the spires continued to blaze with color. Some called this sight the alpenglow, but others, more attuned to enchantment, knew the color for a last lingering trace of Laurin's matchless garden.

Laurin's defeat at the hands of a mortal company was typical of the fates of the dwarf nobility. Honor and magical powers were not enough to secure the knightly dwarfs against the sheer physical vigor of the younger race. The fragile glories of dwarf kingdoms could survive only when they were hidden from mortal sight, as the tale of Laurin witnesses. Yet in those days of trouble and change, enduring bonds sometimes formed between individual dwarfs and mortals of high blood, and great deeds could come of the alliance.

Such a link developed between Otnit, a King of Lombardy, and a dwarf named Alberich. A German tale tells how Otnit desired a wife and summoned his advisers to deliberate the matter. They deemed no maiden fit to share the bed of the noble youth except a certain pagan Princess, a raven-haired beauty who dwelled far across the waves in Syria. Her winning would be a long and perilous quest, for the Sultan, her father, would not willingly accept a Christian suitor.

Otnit's mother begged him not to hazard the attempt. But when she saw that her son was determined, she drew on her knowledge of the byways of enchantment to give him counsel. She told him to ride south, following the path to Rome, until he came to a boulder with a spring chuckling from its base and a linden—a tree that often was the haunt of supernatural beings—standing nearby. There, she said, Otnit would encounter the magical aid by which he would triumph.

He rode south through the meadows and sleepy villages until the scene his mother had described appeared at the roadside: rock, spring, tree and, beneath the tree, a marvel. On the velvety turf lay a small figure clothed in a dazzle of gold and jewels, his pale and delicate features smoothed by sleep.

Otnit pitied the little figure, seemingly a child neglected by his mother, and he stooped to gather him in his arms. Just then the eyes opened, and Otnit backed away from a gaze that was ancient, wise and utterly serene. The Dwarf King—for such a being could have no other identity—rose to his feet and smilingly vowed to punish the mortal for his forwardness. An instant later Otnit found himself in pitched battle with his diminutive opponent, who darted and shimmered like a dragonfly, wielding a sword no bigger than a knitting needle. Yet his strokes were preternaturally heavy, and Otnit was weakening when at last he overcame the pygmy knight and pressed the edge of his sword to the dwarf's throat.

The dwarf declared he would answer no questions while his life was being threatened; but when Otnit sheathed his sword, his foe drew himself up and said that he was Alberich, ruler of a vast but hidden kingdom of dwarfs. As ransom for his life, Alberich would give Otnit a magical sword and suit of armor. And if Otnit would accept him as a comrade in arms, he would offer even more. The dwarf knew of Otnit's quest for the heathen maiden and he would happily render him the aid that would ensure success.

His speech finished, the dwarf clasped hands with the astonished mortal, then twinkled into the shadows at the base of the rock and returned with the ransom. He laid the arms at Otnit's feet, promised to reappear whenever Otnit had need of him and dissolved into the air, his gems leaving behind a stray sparkle that danced in the balmy air for a moment before it, too, winked out.

In the eventful weeks that followed, Otnit saw no more of his magical helper. He mustered an army, marched it south to Messina, in Sicily, and there embarked with his men for the hostile lands to the east. But when the expeditionary force neared the Sultan's port, they found it heavily fortified. Otnit despaired of slipping his fleet past its defenses. Then a thin voice filtered down from the mast of his

The dwarf Alberich, perching high above a galleon's deck, voyaged
to Syria with King Otnit of Lombardy, then supplied a
magic stone that helped his companion woo a pretty, pagan bride.

Protected by invisibility, Alberich roamed the palace of the Syrian Sultan,
    taunting the baffled monarch and entreating his fair daughter to honor Otnit's love.

flagship to reassure him. It was Alberich, who had perched there since the fleet set sail. Still invisible, Alberich slipped down the mast; then he took form at Otnit's side and held out a gaudy pebble for Otnit to slip under his tongue. It would give him the gift of every language, said the dwarf, and with its aid Otnit could impersonate a Syrian merchant and gain free passage into the harbor.

Once the force had landed and set off across the sere plains for the Sultan's capital, Alberich threw himself into Otnit's quest with such relish that the Lombard King himself was eclipsed. Becoming invisible again the dwarf stole into the Sultan's throne room and loudly pressed Otnit's claim; when the Sultan sputtered with rage and declared that he would sooner lose his kingdom than see his daughter married to a Christian, the sportive dwarf leaped up onto the old man's lap and tore out handfuls of his grizzled beard while the Sultan bellowed and groped for his assailant. Then, chuckling and strewing tatters of beard, Alberich left the throne room and fleeted along the battlements, flinging the crossbows and catapults that were the castle's defenses into the waters of the moat.

Finally he encountered the Princess, who watched with a fearful heart as the Sultan's forces assembled for battle. Still invisible, the dwarf told her of the great King from a faraway land who burned with love for her and who was prepared to risk even death to win her hand. He laid a gentle hand on her shoulder and directed her attention to the west, where an army was surging through a gap in the hills. At its

head, in golden armor, with dark hair streaming and lance held high, rode Otnit. The Princess's gaze softened at the sight of the hero who had come questing for her love. Then Alberich knew that the greatest victory was already won.

The Sultan's host was vanquished, and Alberich, with measured words, reminded Otnit and his commanders of their knightly duty to show mercy to their foe. The Sultan was spared, and the pagan Princess happily wedded the conqueror. After hard weeks at sea and a dusty trek up the length of Italy, Otnit and his bride reached the gentle hills of Lombardy and gave themselves over to feasting and rejoicing.

The beneficent dwarf, invisible for so long, took form one last time to join in the happiness he had forged. At the height of the revelry, a hovering focus of crimson light appeared at the center of the hall. As the company fell silent, the point of color crystallized into a ruby, and around the ruby materialized a crown, of which the gem was the centerpiece. At last, beneath the crown, the dwarf himself was revealed. Smiling benignly, he strolled through the company, plucking a sweet melody on a golden harp.

Still playing, he paused at the table of Otnit and his Queen and presented the King with a cloth full of jewels — remuneration for the families that had lost their fathers and husbands in the quest. Then he plucked a final chord, and when the company roused itself from the spell of his playing, Alberich, the bright lord of dwarfish nobility, was gone.

King Herla's Costly Promise

Old as time was the race of dwarfs; their laws were different from those of human-kind, and their miniature kingdoms harbored dangers for mortals ignorant of their ways. So learned Herla, King of the Britons, who struck a bargain with a dwarf and paid dearly for his daring. His adventure began with a boar hunt.

The day was sultry. The sun slowed both hounds and men, and in the afternoon, Herla abandoned his companions for the green shade of a small wood. He stretched out on the grass and thought of cool wine.

No sooner was the thought formed than the King heard rustling in the underbrush. A moment later, a goat appeared among the leaves. Astride the animal was a ruddy-faced, shaggy-haired figure no taller than Herla's knee. A fawnskin adorned the dwarf's shoulders and a king's gold circlet crowned his brow, but his belly and legs were covered only by thick hair, and his feet were cloven hoofs. In his hand he clasped a goblet of gleaming bronze, beaded with droplets of moisture.

"For your thirst, my lord," said the dwarf with a smile as he proffered the drink. King Herla hesitated: Who knew what wine from another world might do? Then, with a shrug, he took the cup.

The Dwarf King watched in silence as Herla drained the goblet. Then the little creature

spoke again to the mortal in his reedy voice: "Now we are companions, King. Let us make a pact of courtesy. I shall attend your wedding when the time for it arrives, and you, in turn, shall come to mine." And Herla agreed.

Within a year, Herla took a wife, and mortal and dwarf met once more. As he had promised, the dwarf appeared at the wedding feast. Into Herla's hall marched the miniature man, leading a company of retainers no larger than himself. The dwarfs played small flutes as they wound through the clustering courtiers, and on their backs they bore precious burdens – gifts of gold for Herla and his bride. These the Dwarf King presented to the mortal with great courtesy, and as he did so, he said these words: "Remember our pact, King Herla, and come to me when I marry."

Herla received the summons one year later. With a company of knights, he rode into the wild country at the fringes of his kingdom, where few men ventured. The track he followed led through dim and ancient forests and ended at the flat face of a limestone cliff. The mortal company halted there, baffled. But in the rock, a seam appeared and widened, and then a door slowly swung open for them. Beyond it, a tunnel led into the earth. With some trepidation, the King and his company followed it, descending ever downward in darkness, until they came to great caverns, whose jewel-spangled walls glittered in the beams of a thousand lanterns. It was the dwarfs' domain, adorned with dwarf-made light for the marriage of its ruler. Generously repaying generosity, Herla offered rich gifts to the Dwarf King and his new Queen, and he joined their wedding feast. After the third day of feasting, Herla prepared to return to his own lands, gathering his company to take leave of the other world. The dwarf's farewell was somber. He placed a tiny hound in Herla's arms.

"You are no longer safe in your own world," said the dwarf. "If you must leave us, heed my words: Let no man dismount his horse before this hound leaps down."

At the gate to the kingdom, horses awaited Herla's company. The animals were fine ones, and richly caparisoned, but they were not Herla's horses. This was a surprise, and the men muttered about it among themselves. At a sign from the King, however, they mounted and rode out of the cavern.

Almost at once, they halted. They were in a strange land. The forest was gone, and in its stead were fields and meadows where fat sheep grazed. Behind the men, the dwarfs' door

swung shut and disappeared; the limestone presented a seamless and silent façade once more. On the track ahead, an elderly shepherd gaped at them.

Herla signaled for quiet and addressed the old man. But the shepherd merely stared and shook his head; he said not a word until Herla spoke his Queen's name. The answer came slowly then, in thickly accented syllables.

"Aye," said the shepherd, "I mind that lady's name. She was a British Queen they tell of, who died of grief when her lord disappeared. But that was centuries ago, in the old days, before we Saxons took the land."

With a shout of terror, one of Herla's men leaped to the ground. And instantly, beginning with his feet, he disintegrated into a cloud of tiny particles, a whole and living man in a moment gone to dust.

Thus King Herla discovered the price of careless bargains. He had tarried too long in the other world, where time passed differently from mortal time: In the hall of the Dwarf King, each day lasted a hundred years. Now Herla was a ghost in his own world, doomed to ride forever – or fade to the dust he had become – unless the dwarf dog leaped to the ground. But the dog never leaped. For long centuries, Herla and his knights haunted the English countryside, a restless band of shades from a vanished age.

Chapter Three

An Ancient Race in Retreat

In the lingering twilight of a summer's day many centuries ago, a Danish peasant pushed open a gate in a wattle fence and surveyed his new homestead. The farm had long been empty, and the home field before the cottage was thick with wild flowers. Here and there the tattered thatch of the cottage roof gaped to show rafters, and the cowshed door hung askew from rusted hinges. The new tenant had come on orders from the district landlord. Previous occupants had brought the lord no profit; disease had thinned their herds, and drought had withered their crops. The newcomer knew of the farm's dismal legacy, and he regarded the decayed buildings morosely. "Well, good evening, farm," he said at last, cutting at the flanks of his packhorse with a switch to urge it through the gate. Just then a voice, as toneless as the croak of a toad, mimicked him. "Good evening," it said, seeming to come from a billow of greenery near the cowshed. The farmer paused again, alert and listening. Only cricket song rose from the green field. He shrugged, then added, on a whim, "Whoever you are, come to the cottage at Christmas and show yourself."

The tenant soon forgot the mysterious greeting, for there was much to occupy him. He patched walls and rethatched the roof, he laid in hay for the winter, he drove his animals to their new pastures, and he summoned his wife and children. One of his cows went dry soon after he had stabled the herd in the cowshed, as if the farm's misfortunes were continuing. But there was salt meat enough for the winter. And on Christmas Eve, when candlelight danced in the frosted windowpanes and the family feasted on goose and ale, the invisible neighbor showed himself.

The door flew open, admitting a chill blast, an eddy of snowflakes and, like a dry leaf whirling in the wind, a beaming dwarf. As the visitor shut the door, the children gaped and their mother shrieked, but the farmer rose to greet the little man. He was as gnarled and glossy as a polished oak burl, his broad face was fringed with a white beard, and he wore gray padded winter clothes and a red stocking cap. When he wished the family the best of holidays, the farmer recognized the voice that had greeted him the summer before.

The peasant offered him a stool and a plate of goose, and the dwarf balanced the food on his knees and chewed noisily while the children watched wide-eyed. After he had finished, he swung down from the stool and bowed deeply. "And now you must allow me to return the favor," he said. "Come to the cowshed on New Year's Eve, and you will not fail to meet me." Then he whirled out into the night.

The farmer was chary of dealings with a supernatural being, but he feared to insult the dwarf. On New Year's Eve he waded through the drifts to the shed, where he waited in the gloom. Soon he felt a touch, and he looked down to see the dwarf, pale in the moonlight filtering through the shed's single window. Behind the dwarf was a hole ringed with loose dirt, leading into the hard-packed earth floor. The man's unease grew: The hole was no wider than a badger's burrow; even his boots would not fit into it. But the dwarf led him to the border of fresh earth, released his hand and dropped noiselessly down the dark opening. The farmer, thinking it folly, nevertheless put one foot in the burrow—and slipped into the earth as easily as if he had blundered over the top of a mine shaft.

With a stinging jolt and a hail of clods, he alighted in a low chamber smelling of earth and festooned with roots. Oil lamps cast a yellow glow from niches in the clay walls. The dwarf, with a smile, led him to a table, where a steaming bowl of porridge waited, a pat of butter softening in it.

As the farmer took up a spoon and be-
gan to eat, the dwarf grimaced and gestured upward. At that instant a drop of moisture swelled free of the fissured ceiling and spattered on the table. It was brown and acrid-smelling. The farmer looked inquiringly at the dwarf, whose features had twisted into a scowl.

"Do you see now why no tenant has ever gotten on at this farm?" asked the dwarf. "The first to cultivate the land built the cowshed over my chamber, and ever since its muddy floor has oozed through my ceiling and ruined my food." In the sullen silence that followed this declaration, the farmer heard the muted stamping and lowing of his own stock directly overhead. "I bear malice to no mortal," continued the dwarf, "but in my rage at spoiled porridge I have many times blighted a tenant's crops or cursed his cattle. I advise you to move the cowshed when the thaw comes, so that we both may prosper."

Cheered that he might fare better than his predecessors, the peasant agreed. When he had eaten, the dwarf led him to tiny stairs cut in the burrow's wall. He began to climb, and the passage broadened miraculously, slipping easily past his shoulders. But it narrowed again as he emerged into the darkness of the shed, and he had to wrench his boot free of the earth. Bursting with news, he returned to his family. When the snows melted, he summoned sturdy young men from nearby farms, and after a day's work the old cowshed was reduced to a pile of timbers and a patch of foul-smelling mud. During a second day's labor, the shed rose again on the far side of the cot-

tage. And the farm's misfortunes ended. The dry cow soon gave abundant milk, and in his healthy beasts and bountiful harvests, the farmer saw that the dwarf's ill will had changed to benison.

Such was the intimacy that flourished in those days between dwarfs and the peasantry of northern Europe. The names given to the race of little people varied from land to land, as did details of their appearance, but everywhere dwarfs dwelled in or very near the peasants' world of village, field, forest and mountain. Although dwarfs were rarely met, their influence touched matters that lay at the center of the peasants' existence: agriculture and the humble crafts of spinning, smithing, brewing, baking and cheese making.

Some farmfolk believed that it was from dwarfs that their forebears first learned such skills, long before history began. For the dwarfs of the countryside were a supernatural peasantry, their ways a magical likeness of the peasants' own. People in other walks of life learned of heroic dwarfs, such as Laurin and Alberich, from tales declaimed by wandering singers in courts and village squares. But countryfolk knew of their dwarfish neighbors from incidents of their daily lives, and much of what they knew was eminently familiar.

Yet the parallels between dwarfs and mortal peasants were by no means perfect. There were differences that both sides felt keenly as they strove to maintain the happy relations essential to their coexistence. The dwarfs were an old tribe, shy and conservative, possessors of wisdom that sprang from ancient acquaintance with the soil. By some accounts, they were the first race to populate the meadows and knolls of the newly shaped earth, and they regarded the mortal newcomers with the ambivalence of an aboriginal people. Their interactions with mortals were frequent, yet dwarfs hung back from full view. They remained reserved and secretive, often going about their business cloaked in invisibility. Humanity's clamorous and expansive ways, its addiction to novelty and growth, seemed to pain them.

Reclusive, fretful and seemingly weakened by the great age of their race, dwarfs nonetheless commanded the power to awe their mortal neighbors. The little people guarded mysteries that mortals, for all their restless, searching ways, could never comprehend. It was easy for humans to underestimate their quiet neighbors, but to do so was dangerous. Dwarfs quickly brought to heel any who trifled with them.

One victim of their anger was a shepherd who, along with a friend, pastured his flock near the Danish coast. He and his companion were idling near their sheep when a summer rainstorm blustered in from the North Sea. They sought shelter at the base of a sandstone crag that overlooked the meadow. A hollow undercut the crag, and as they crawled out of the rain, they saw a passage, no wider than a man's shoulders, leading deeper into the rock. The sand at its mouth was dimpled with small footprints, and from the opening curled a wisp of smoke.

Then the shepherds remembered tales told on winter evenings in their village. Late at night, it was said, when the meadows were empty, small gray men spilled from that rock like windborne dust, swirling in moonlit dances. Sometimes they carried treasures – filigree of silver and tapestries woven with threads of gold – to shake and air them in the sea breeze.

Those remembered tales of treasure spurred the bolder shepherd. He told his companion that he wanted to explore the passage, and he discounted his friend's objections, agreeing only to fasten one end of a rope around his waist and let the other lad pay out slack as he ventured into the rock. He held a lighted candle before his face, wedged himself headfirst into the narrow opening, wriggled and was gone.

At first the rope slipped briskly through the palms of the waiting shepherd. Then it stopped. Through its taut length, he felt a far-off tremor. From the dark opening, he heard a cry, faint as a kitten's mew, and the rope went slack. To see if his friend was still there, the lad twitched the line; it slithered toward him with sickening ease.

Panicked now, the shepherd hauled in the rope, and soon its free end whipped from the opening. There was no trace of his friend, and only a cryptic sign of his fate: The rope was charred, and smoke still rose from the seared hemp. The shepherd gazed for a moment, pierced with horror, then fled home through the driving rain. His friend was never seen again.

But such tales of dwarfs' demonic powers were rare. The dwarfish power that most fascinated the peasants was a sunnier kind of magic: an ability to conjure riches. Dwarf-given gold was as cold and dense as any coin of the realm, but it was born of enchantment. Through their power over the earth's mineral riches, dwarfs accumulated stocks of treasure within their burrows; they also, when the occasion warranted, could transform the most mundane elements – coal and candlewax, among others – to gold and jewels.

Most astonishing of all, to their poor peasant neighbors, was the capriciousness of their largess. Sometimes a farmer was richly rewarded after doing a dwarf a good turn; sometimes the dwarfs' generosity seemed a matter of happenstance.

Among those inexplicably blessed was a simple Danish girl, more bold than prudent. One Sunday in early spring, she made her way home from church along a sodden path through fields that were patchy with mud and thinning snow. The girl stepped gingerly among the puddles, careful of her Sunday frills, but as her path skirted a hummock at one end of a field the hill's flank seemed to twitch.

She stopped and stared. It was the south side of the mound that had caught her eye, and she now saw that its mantle of snow had melted. Here and there, matted tufts of brown grass were exposed, but everywhere else the surface of the mound quivered with animal life. It teemed with iridescent green scarab beetles, creeping and tumbling in the warm sunlight.

The hillock was said to be a haunt of *bergfolk* – the mound-dwelling dwarfs of Denmark – the extraordinary beetles might be part of their magic. It was a spectacle to report to her family, but only if they saw the creatures would they believe the girl's account. She therefore approached the twitching net of insects, carefully untangled two of the beetles and dropped them in her woolen glove. Then she pocketed the glove and went on her way.

The beetles stirred in her coat pocket at first, but by the time she reached her parents' farm they were still. She forgot her tale until the Sunday meal was over and her father and brothers sat by the hearth, gossiping. When she described what she had seen, they scoffed and told her that her shimmering scarabs were nothing more than the sparkle of meltwater.

There was nothing for it but to produce the beetles. The glove felt heavy as she pulled it from her coat. She shook it over the flagstones. No beetles appeared; instead, two heavy gold pieces clattered onto the hearth. The girl gazed at more wealth than peasants saw in an ordinary season. Then she crowed: "Those were beetles—bergmen's magical beetles!"

But her kinsmen were tripping over benches in their haste to reach the door. They splashed to the mound, hopeful of a

harvest of beetles. Soon, however, they came dragging back, hands and pockets empty. The dwarfs had gathered in their beetles before the tantalized mortals arrived, and the flank of the mound lay bare.

Tales of dwarfish wizardry, both demonic and beneficent, terrified and intrigued their hearers. But the dwarfs that most peasants knew rarely displayed such powers. Instead, they trained quieter magic on the tasks of craftsman, housewife and farmer, sometimes hindering but more often helping their mortal neighbors.

Such modest favors risked going unappreciated. In Switzerland, where peasants tilled the fertile valleys, dwarfs dwelled in the rockfalls that spilled down the high slopes. Reclusive beings, they whistled, marmot-like, in warning when a mortal strayed into their domain. But when autumn gilded the larches and the grain ripened, the dwarfs emerged. As the sun sank below the peaks each evening, they sat on their rocks, watching shadows march across the valley floors and hearth fires flicker in cottage windows as the men returned from the fields.

When the peasants were closed in their dwellings, the dwarfs seized tiny scythes and rakes and pelted down the mountainsides into the fields. Sturdy and shapeless, clothed in stout homespun, they scythed and raked and bound the grain in the moonlight. As they worked, they chattered in thin voices that sleepless peasants sometimes mistook for songbirds' twitter. When dawn touched the peaks, they shouldered their implements and fled back to their rocky redoubts, leaving the sheaves scattered on the stubble.

Most years the peasants were grateful for the harvest help. Guessing that the dwarfs waited just inside the shadows of the rockfalls to hear how their kindness was received, the peasants whooped and shouted when they rose the next morning, praising their kind, industrious neighbors. When, far above, the dwarfs heard the distant clamor, they flushed with pleasure, and the happy ritual was complete.

One year, though, the peasants in a remote valley rose on a summer morning, weeks before harvest time, to find that their grain had been scythed down to stubble. Bound in sheaves, the unripe grain littered the fields. The premature harvest was clearly the work of the dwarfs. Although the peasants did not wish to offend their helpers, they could not bring themselves to thank them. Grim-faced, the men traversed the fields with oxcarts, loading the sheaves to carry them to the floor of the threshing barn, where they would have no easy time trying to free the unripe grain from the straw.

But not long after the men had hauled away the last cartload, thunderclouds boiled over the peaks at the head of the valley, and as the storm drove down toward the village, its sheets of rain changed to hail. When the peasants in their cottages no longer heard the rustle of hailstones beating on the thatch and judged that the storm's fury was past, they ventured outdoors and saw their fields thickly pebbled with ice. It was clear that the prescient dwarfs had saved the harvest and spared the people a hungry winter.

The kindly Swiss dwarfs seemed content with the peasants' thanks, and many other tales record dwarfs' cheerful, unrequited favors. In some districts, however, their activity took on the character of an exchange—a furtive commerce in articles and aid. Almost always, the trade favored the mortals, for the dwarfs' magical powers made their contributions disproportionately generous.

At a farm on the fringe of England's Dartmoor, for instance, a band of pixies—the dwarfs of that region—once set about threshing the wheat harvest. Night after night the swat of tiny flails sounded inside the threshing barn, and every morning the farmer entered the deserted building to take stock of the growing heap of grain and the neatly bundled and stacked straw from which it had been threshed. As payment, he left bread and cheese every day at one corner of the threshing floor.

So the exchange continued, day after day, until the farmer realized that the pixy helpers had long since threshed the last of his harvest. But that night, too, the noise of pixy flails filtered from the barn, and the farmer could only conclude that the dwarfs were threshing ripe grain from thin air. Yet he was not one to shun good fortune. He kept up the payments of bread and cheese, and the pixies continued their magical threshing until the farmer's storeroom bulged with surplus.

Such tales suggested that dwarfs regarded peasants' payments for their aid as little more than tokens of gratitude. Peasants had little to offer but coarse food, and surely beings who could conjure up enough grain to burst a granary had no need for black bread and rank cheese. Yet the appearance of exchange was no illusion: By most accounts, dwarfs valued and even depended on the peasants' offerings.

Perhaps dwarfs found the products of their enchantments unwholesome – although mortals rarely suffered ill effects from the bounty they received from dwarfs. Or perhaps dwarf charms were a fitful source of sustenance. Whatever the case, it seemed clear that dwarfs, like mortals, ordinarily sustained themselves through humble toil. It was known, for instance, that Swiss dwarfs herded flocks of chamois, from whose milk they made a hard, fragrant cheese, and that dwarf wom-

Friends to the farmer, shy Swiss dwarfs worked in secret under the harvest moon, reaping and tying and bringing in the sheaves as the humans slept.

en baked bread underground, in ovens identical to those of mortal housewives.

But goats could go dry and bread could fail to rise, as peasants knew well from their own uncertain lives; like them, dwarfs sometimes ran short of essentials. Like ordinary countryfolk, they appealed to their mortal neighbors for loans of food, to be repaid in kind. But even so prosaic an exchange between a dwarf and a mortal could be touched with magic, as a Danish farmwife discovered.

One evening the woman sat alone beside the fire, spinning; her husband was away, and she did not expect him back for several days. Her reverie was broken

by a knock. Before she had time to rise, the door creaked open and a face, round and ruddy as a beet, peered in. Then a stunted little woman in a peasant's full skirts stumped in, filling the air with the smell of freshly turned earth.

The mortal woman started up, but the dwarf reproached her: "Do you not know me? We have been neighbors for many years—I with my people in the mound at the forest's edge, you here among your kind. But no matter. We have run short of ale. Could you spare a barrel?"

The woman, eager to help, led the bergwoman outside to a storage shed and tipped a small cask of ale from a high shelf. She set it before the dwarf, who seized her hand in her own calloused palms and thanked her effusively. As the farmwife returned to her fire, she heard the barrel rumbling along the rough lane. The dwarf was rolling it back to her thirsty people in the mound.

Several nights later, there was again a knock at the door. The farmwife flung it open. On the step stood the dwarf woman, her small round shoulders heaving with the effort of wrestling an ale barrel up to the threshold. "I have returned to you all you lent me, and more," she said. "But remember that this cask will prove most bountiful if you never look inside it." Then she pattered off down the lane.

The woman carried the barrel out to the shed and hefted it onto the shelf, and she thought no more about it until her husband returned and the haymaking began. Each day the workers trailed in from the fields flushed and fiercely thirsty, and soon the farmwife tapped the bergwoman's ale barrel. The brew was heady and exquisitely bitter, and the flow did not slacken through the month of haying.

From time to time, the woman knocked on the sides of the barrel to determine how much ale remained. She could detect no lowering of the level. At last her curiosity won out: With mallet and chisel she pried open the cask. She tipped the container, grown suddenly lighter, and when she peered into it her spirits sank. It was empty, its sides quilted with mold and curtained with cobwebs. She clapped the lid back on the barrel and left it for two days, hoping that the magical ale would renew itself. But the barrel stayed dry, and at last she broke it up and used it for kindling.

But the dwarf woman's debt had been repaid many times over. On such friendly exchanges, on mutual aid in matters of sustenance and handicraft, a happy alliance developed between peasants and dwarfs. Commerce often became routine, as in districts where the local smith was not a mortal but a dwarf, plying the trade of his ancestors. A peasant in need of a scythe or a plowshare would set a lump of iron and a coin at the base of a knoll known to shelter dwarfs, shout his request at the dumb flank of the mound, and leave. The next morning, the coin would be gone, and in the place of the iron would be a newly forged steel blade.

Nor was the traffic always so furtive, for bonds of intimacy sometimes sprang up between mortals and dwarfs. In Germany, it was said that a dwarf once took pity on a tattered, homeless girl who dragged her-

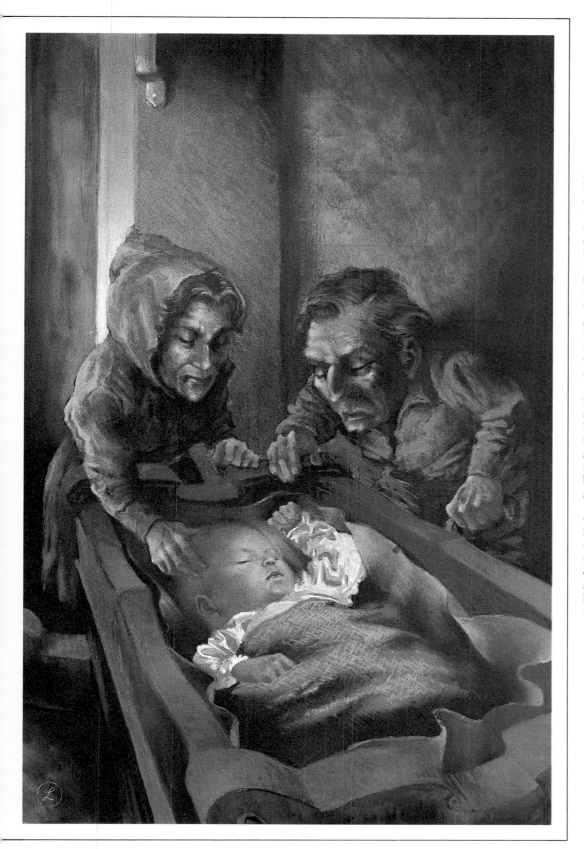

Cradle thieves in quest of vigor

Dwarfs, it seemed, had need of mortal blood, for countryfolk reported that children were sometimes stolen from them and changelings – old and weakened dwarfs – left in their place. The child at risk, said wise folk, was a newborn who had not yet been christened, whose cradle was not protected by a piece of iron or bread – both defenses against creatures of the other world – and whose slumber was not guarded by the parents. Such a child might well receive small visitors at night, a dwarf woman, perhaps, who would creep into the chamber leading a fragile elder of her tribe by the hand. In a twinkling, the change would be made. The child would be spirited away to the dwarfs' world, far from its home, and in the morning, the mortal mother would find the impostor – a grotesque creature, querulous and demanding – in place of her own rosy baby. She would have become the guardian of an aged dwarf.

The dwarf would not speak, but he would wail – fractiously and constantly – and the mortal mother would be trapped, unless she could frighten or fool him into speaking. If the small creature spoke, thus revealing himself as no mortal infant, he had to return to his own kind, and restore the mortal infant to its rightful mother.

A grateful dwarf's gift was fine indeed, for it was usually touched by magic. One such offering was an ale cask that never ran dry—until the recipient peered inside.

self past his mound. From behind a screen of matted grass and wild flowers, he called to her, then drew back the curtain of greenery to show her into the cave, where treasures glittered from earthen niches. He fed her cakes and milk and, overcome by her humility and grace, asked her to marry him. By all accounts, their union was a happy one. Another kind of intimacy was more common, one that began with a frantic rapping at the door of a midwife. There would stand a dwarf, dancing with agitation, seeking the skilled hands of a mortal midwife to ease his wife through labor.

But the trust and harmony that grew up between mortals and dwarfs was a fragile thing. The greatest threat to it was the dwarfs' sensitivity. They were a prideful race, easily wounded, and when they saw a slight they became aloof or hostile.

Mortals who spurned dwarfs' gifts were sure to feel their wrath, as a Danish tale shows. It recounts the events of a spring day on a farm in the north of Jutland, the peninsula that makes up much of Denmark. In that region, featureless marsh and heath then stretched to the horizon, interrupted only by scattered farms and, here and there, a low hummock.

Such a mound stood at the end of a long field, fallow and weed-grown, which two farmhands were plowing in preparation for spring planting. One guided the heavy plow; the other ambled beside the ox, idly swatting it to urge it along. As they approached the far end of the field, a rich odor of baking bread seemed to waft from the mound, but the men thought nothing of it until the ox driver noticed a tiny shovel lying on the tussocky slope of the knoll. While his companion wrestled the ox and the plow into position to turn the next furrow, the driver ran to pick up the shovel.

It was a bread shovel, used for retrieving loaves from an oven. But no mortal baker owned the implement, for it was the size of a human's serving spoon. It was also broken, its paddle splintered away from its handle. The lads guessed what had happened: Within the mound, a bergwoman tending her oven had reached for her shovel when her loaves were done. She had found it broken and useless, and now she was counting on the farmhands' kindness.

While his companion leaned on the plow handles and watched, the ox driver searched through his pockets for nails, then plucked two stones from the furrow: a flat one to support his work and an egg-shaped one as a hammer. Gently, he nailed the paddle back to the slender shaft, then replaced the shovel where he had found it among the tussocks.

"Now we shall want some bread for our trouble," said the plowman as his friend coaxed the ox forward. His companion, however, only shrugged.

For her part, the dwarf was glad to reward them, as they discovered when, many minutes later, they pushed their furrow to the far end of the field once again. The shovel had vanished, and in its place was a folded napkin, with steam curling from it. The ox driver hurried over to the cloth and chortled with pleasure when he unfolded it to reveal two fist-sized loaves of bread, hot and fragrant.

It was nearing midday, and he seized one loaf and chewed it hungrily. But when he offered the other to his companion, the plowman, who had been so avid for a reward, drew back. He was not hungry, he said, and besides, you never knew what unwholesome taints of earth and mold and magic a dwarf's bread might contain. He would rather keep his loaf as a souvenir, to show the dairymaids at suppertime. And he slipped the loaf into his pocket.

As the men drove the ox back toward the barn after the day's plowing, they remembered the bergwoman, and the plowman ridiculed his companion for trustingly eating her bread. Delighted with himself for disdaining it, he pulled the loaf from his pocket and tossed it high in the air, catching and hurling it again and again as he capered down the lane, whooping and jeering.

Yet it was he, not his quiet companion, who left the supper table early that evening, pale and stricken. During the night he tossed and cried out, and in the morning the other farmhands awoke to the sound of a struggle. The plowman lay uncovered on his pallet, thrashing and foaming about the mouth. But before they could reach him, his shuddering limbs had gone limp forever.

Genial as they were in the course of their ordinary relations with peasantry, dwarfs gave no quarter to mortals who, like this plowman, were churlish or unjust. Even the humblest of dwarfs retained the power to strike down mortals for their wrongs—a lesson made brutally clear in a Swiss mountain hamlet.

That story began when a dwarf entered the village on a night of gusty rain. Water streamed from his beard, and his forest green clothing clung to his squat body. He splashed through the rivulets that veined the lane, knocking on door after door in search of shelter. At each, the ruddy peasant who answered, warm with soup and beer, looked down at the bedraggled dwarf on his doorstep—humpbacked, thick-featured and smelling of the forest—and shut the door with a bang.

But at the last house of the village, an old man, as piteously bent as the dwarf himself, unbolted the door. As his fragile wife hovered behind him, smiling, he welcomed the dwarf into his cottage.

The old woman fluttered about, fetching bread and cheese and a cloth for the dwarf's sodden face and beard, while her husband drew an extra stool up to the hearth. The visitor sat for a time in silence while color returned to his cheeks and his boots steamed gently from the heat of the fire. At last, as the rain slackened, the dwarf rose. He thanked the old couple for their kindness, but said that he must be on his way. When the old pair objected, offering him a bed for the night, he shook his head. "I have urgent business on the mountainside tonight. By morning you will understand, and you will know that I have not forgotten your kindness."

Soon after the door closed behind the dwarf, the storm returned with redoubled fury. Toward morning, the drumming of the rain grew fitful, and during the pauses the sleepless villagers heard rushing water. When they rubbed the fog from their windowpanes and peered out into the gloom they saw that the lane had become a torrent, roiling with flotsam.

As a blood red dawn broke between thunderclouds and gray peaks, a distant rumble drew the villagers onto their doorsteps. Water still streamed down the lane, but the villagers' fear was not of this local freshet but of a river far up the valley, which had been known to burst its banks.

They clutched one another in fear as a great wind began to blow through the valley. Then the trees above the village bowed and vanished as a brown wall of water appeared, tumbling beasts and torn branches on its foamy crest. Hurtling down upon them, it swallowed up the villagers and their cottages. But at the far end of the hamlet, the old couple cowering before their cottage noticed something extraordinary. Bowling along at the head of the flood was a barn-sized boulder, and atop it, dancing to keep his footing, was the dwarf whom the couple had sheltered the night before. No longer bent, he now stood erect and squatly powerful, and he grasped the trunk of a stout fir. He trailed it in the floodwaters like a tiller, twitching it this way and that to steer the boulder straight for the old couple.

As the careering boulder and the tide of water were almost upon them, the dwarf lifted the trunk, whirled it high over the boulder and plunged it into the earth. The rock fetched up against the trunk and shuddered to a halt. The waters were parted, and they streamed harmlessly around the cottage of the kindhearted old pair. And while the couple watched in amazement and gratitude, the dwarf swelled until he bestrode the valley and his smiling visage darkened the sky. Then he thinned into mist and vanished. Of all the peasants in that mountain hamlet, only the old man and his wife were left to tell the tale.

And a curious tale it was—that a dwarf could be prey to hunger, cold and weariness, yet possess such godlike powers. Still, contradictions had been part of the nature of dwarfs since earliest times. Their capacity to be both pathetic and potent, both wise and foolish, had been demonstrated countless times. And countryfolk were well aware of another contradiction: Dwarfs championed virtue in their mortal neighbors, but they too were prone to a multitude of foibles.

Accounts of dwarfs' misdeeds disagree about their motives. In some instances, dwarfs seemed driven by an irrepressible sense of mischief; in others, by dire necessity—the same material needs that led them to trade with the peasantry. Although countryfolk whispered dark tales of mortal

Safe in their earthen mound houses, the bergfolk of Denmark watched the human world go by. But they knew when to solicit assistance: If, for example, a dwarf woman broke a baking tool, she might turn to mortal neighbors for repairs.

Mortal cruelty wrought dwarfish cruelty, mortal goodness dwarfish good. Once, a kind mortal couple who had aided a dwarf were repaid when the little man lodged a boulder in front of their cottage and diverted the waters of a raging flood.

babies stolen from their cribs and replaced with ailing dwarf children or frail oldsters, the most common of dwarf wrongs was the stealing of crops, bread and ale.

In many tales it is clear that dwarfs did not willingly turn to crime, for when they were discovered they were heartily sorry. In the Harz Mountains, a forested region of Germany, an otherwise-prosperous peasant found each year that his harvest of apricots and peas fell short of his expectations. Just as the apricots ripened and the pea pods swelled, ready for picking, the orchard and the pea patch seemed to lose a portion of their bounty overnight.

One summer night, after a season of gentle rain and warm sunshine that seemed certain to yield a fine harvest, a knock roused the farmer. At his door stood a frightened wayfarer, whispering that spirits were afoot in the fields and groves.

The farmer pulled on his breeches and hurried out, and in the moonlight he saw that invisible invaders were despoiling his crops. Pea pods were flying off the plants and gathering in piles amid the furrows. In the orchard, the lowest boughs of his apricot trees danced and trembled, although the night was calm. As he watched, the branches shed their burden of apricots, which slipped to the earth as slowly as golden bubbles. The farmer had a countryman's respect for spirits, but he could not restrain himself. He raced among the trees, cursing, and the apricots that hung in midair showered leadenly to the ground. There was a patter of footsteps. Then the orchard and pea patch were still.

The next day, the farmer told his tale to a wise woman of the village, and that night he acted on her advice. Grasping a willow switch, he hid in the bushes at the edge of the pea patch. Soon the field was alive with predatory activity once again. Pods flickered from the plants as invisible hands worked with marvelous efficiency. The farmer sprang from the shadows, whooping and flailing the air at waist height with his willow switch. All around him sounded a frantic chittering. He lunged in every direction, swinging ferociously, and twice the switch struck something soft. Then he heard thin voices pleading for mercy.

Two dwarfs knelt in the dirt, their bare pates, fringed with silvery hair, bowed under the moonlight. Their peaked red caps lay out of reach among the furrows, swatted from their heads by the farmer's switch. It was as the wise woman had said: The thieves were dwarfs, and once deprived of their magical caps they were visible and powerless to escape.

The captives were too shamefaced and dispirited even to try. Weeping, they confessed that their tribe had stolen from the farmer each year, but only out of the direst need. Their own herds and gardens no longer sustained them, and their magic often failed them in moments of want.

The farmer listened, unswayed to mercy. He was not a hard man, but he had suffered long and grievously from the dwarfs' thieving, and he was determined to profit from his present advantage. He picked up the red caps and stuffed them in his pockets, then ordered the dwarfs to their feet. Waving his willow switch, he marched the dwarfs back to the farm and locked them in an outbuilding.

The next morning, envoys from the dwarf tribe arrived on his doorstep, tattered and downcast, to bargain for their comrades' release. The farmer demanded ransom and led the dwarfs into his parlor to dicker. But soon there were other, stouter knocks at the door. Other peasants of the district had come to press their own claims against the dwarfs, for all had seen their harvests mysteriously thinned, season after season. Their position was harsh: They demanded nothing less than the departure of the dwarf tribe.

Perched on stools at the center of the crowd of angry farmers, the dwarf envoys grew ever more dejected as the accusations flew. In the end they agreed to leave the district, and they added that the journey would take the tribe across a footbridge that spanned a stream to the north of the village. If the villagers would place a caldron at one end of the bridge, each dwarf would toss in a piece of treasure as he passed, to compensate the people of the Harz for their losses.

On the appointed day, curious peasants gathered on the grassy bank of the stream, dressed in their festive best and chattering gaily. Then the narrow, split-log bridge began to creak and shudder, and the crowd fell silent. There was nothing to see; the dwarfs were shielded from mortal sight by their caps. But the invisible procession continued for many minutes, and mixed with the groan of the timbers was the ringing of gold pieces tossed one by one into the caldron that stood at the far end of the bridge.

At last nothing sounded but the chuckle of the stream and the hiss of the wind in the pines, and the peasants' mood darkened. A subtle but comforting presence had passed out of their world, and the woods and meadows seemed barren.

It was a scene that was repeated in all the lands where dwarfs resided. At some point in the history of every district, the fragile harmony between dwarfs and mortals came unstrung, and the dwarfs abandoned their haunts en masse, rarely revealing their destination. The reasons for their exodus varied, however, and in that respect the episode in the Harz Mountains was unusual. More often, it was mortals rather than dwarfs who were at fault.

In many cases the dwarfs fled from humanity's mounting vigor and appetite for change. In their natural conservatism, dwarfs were pained by any alteration in the landscape or in the ways of their human neighbors. The clearing of forests, the growth of towns, new means of harrowing the soil—across a field rather than down its length—all grated on the sensibilities of dwarfs, and each could be sufficient cause for their departure.

In other instances, dwarfs cited the noise as their reason for fleeing populous districts. But peasants suspected that the dwarfs objected less to the disturbance itself than to what it signified. Noise was the hallmark of human expansiveness. The clatter of forges and weavers' looms, the shouts of children, the pealing church bells of new congregations—all heralded a future in which dwarfs, creatures of the placid countryside, could have no part.

Mockery drove dwarfs from humankind. When a Swiss farmer discovered
that his little neighbors had webbed feet, he hooted with derision. The wounded
dwarfs then vanished from the region and aided the farmer at harvest no more.

In still other districts, dwarfs recoiled from the wickedness of the countryfolk — not a new aspect of life, but one that became more obtrusive with the growth of the populace. Sometimes the mere spectacle of mortal iniquity was enough to send dwarfs fleeing, but more often the trigger was a direct affront. The dwarfs in one Alpine valley of Switzerland took offense when a disrespectful shepherd pried into their secrets. It happened like this:

Outside the shepherd's stone hut in a forest-fringed meadow stood a cherry tree, gnarled and ancient, which every year grew heavy with fruit. The tree's bounty was sweetened by the fact that it harvested itself: The shepherd, following the custom of his father and grandfather, simply placed baskets under the boughs every year when the fruit ripened, and overnight the boughs shed their fat crimson cherries directly into the baskets.

Or so it seemed. In fact, said villagers to whom he described his remarkable tree one day when he drove his sheep to market, the shepherd was blessed with kindly harvest helpers — dwarfs. All over the valley, said the townsfolk, dwarfs streamed from the forest in the still of the night to aid the shepherds and farmers, tripping along in cloaks so long that no mortal had ever seen a dwarf's feet.

The shepherd was entranced by the thought of the dwarfs' nocturnal industry, silent and unobserved — and he was consumed with curiosity about their feet. He wondered what horror or deformity they might be hiding under their cloaks, and although fearful of offending the helpful spirits, he determined to find out. That year, when the ripening cherries hung heavy on the boughs, he conceived a plan.

It would soon be time for the dwarfs to visit the tree, and when he set out the cherry baskets to receive the harvest he also carried a bucket of ash from his hearth. Chuckling to himself, he dipped into the bucket with a spoon and sprinkled ash in a fine shower all around the base of the tree, whitening the soil. Then he went home to wait for morning.

The next day he hurried out into the bright dawn. The tree was bare of fruit, and the baskets overflowed. And patterning the pale ash were the wedge-shaped prints of innumerable goose feet. The shepherd gaped, then guffawed, and he hurried down the forest path toward the village, eager to spread the news. That afternoon, he returned with a crowd of curious villagers. He led them to the telltale prints in the ash, and they set the mountainsides ringing with derisive laughter.

Then the onlookers fell silent. For from the slopes high above pealed a cry of anguish. The mortals knew that their offense had been grave, and the crowd broke up, abashed and gloomy, and filed back to their homes in the village.

They had lost more than the dwarfs' good will, as they soon discovered. From that day on, the high slopes of scree that bounded the valley were deserted, and the surreptitious favors that had brightened the peasants' existence were at an end. The dwarfs who had populated the region from the earliest days were gone. And as for the foolish shepherd, each season he

In time, all the dwarf tribes left the mortal world, sad refugees from the growing clamor.

Where they went no one could tell, save that the way was hard and the shores were distant.

lost half his cherries to birds before he could finish the harvest.

Compared with some, his was a mild affront; in other instances, dwarfs fled not ill-mannered curiosity and ridicule but outright cruelty. The dwarfs of a neighboring valley liked to perch, invisible, on a great rock overlooking the fields during the haymaking. But their excited twitter betrayed them as they watched mortals flirt and fight and quaff ale during those frenetic days, when the entire village took to the fields to mow and dry hay for the winter. Prankish lads one night lighted a fire on the perch, let it burn until the rock shimmered with heat, then swept away the coals. When the unsuspecting dwarfs arrived the next morning to take up their vantage, they burned themselves grievously. With piercing shrieks, they fled back to their underground homes, and soon afterward they marched away.

The exodus of a dwarf troop usually took place screened from mortal view by night or by the dwarfs' own invisibility, but one mortal was privileged to glimpse the sad event. His name was Reimer, and he was a ferryman.

Reimer lived at a time when the isolation of Europe was ending. Coaches rattled from town to town along roads that cut through once-trackless forests; factories supplied cloth and tools that had come from housewives' looms and village smithies; and the population of country districts began to feel the trammels of a centralized state.

To continue plying his ferry route across the Lim Fjord, a sound in northern Jutland, Reimer had to obtain a license from a bureau in Copenhagen, the capital of Denmark, many days' journey to the south. He completed this business just before Christmas, and on Christmas Eve he wandered the slushy streets of the capital, wincing at the bright glare of the gaslights and the noisy cheer of the revelers, and pining for his snug cottage on the lonely shore of the sound.

He felt a touch on his leg and looked down into searching eyes and a wizened face. It was a stunted old man, wearing a long, skirted coat and riding boots. Although Reimer had never seen him before, the old man addressed him by name and made a proposition: If Reimer would agree to ferry a large cargo across the Lim Fjord, the dwarf would carry him home to his family that very night.

Reimer had no objections, although he had little faith that the dwarf could do as he promised. Wordlessly, the little man led him through the winding streets and out the city gates. Tethered to a pine tree just beyond the wall was a glossy black horse, no higher than Reimer's hip. The old man untied the creature and mounted, and Reimer, fearful for the horse's back, gingerly climbed on behind. His feet stayed planted in the snow as he straddled the little animal, but when spurs flashed on the old man's heels and the horse lurched into motion, Reimer was startled to feel his feet dangle freely.

He closed his eyes in terror as the landscape dropped away, towns and woods dwindling to patches of darkness on the pale expanse of snow. A great wind beat in his face, then abated, and Reimer's feet were jolted by solid ground. The horse had alighted, and the ferryman opened his eyes on his own cottage, its windows festively aglow with candles. The old man turned and smiled benignly, and Reimer backed away from a being he now knew was no ordinary old man but a dwarf.

In the elation of his homecoming, Reimer forgot his half of the bargain. Two nights later, however, when the Christmas feasting was finished, the dwarf knocked at the door to summon him. Now solemn, holding a red woolen cap in his hands and wearing shapeless gray robes, the dwarf told Reimer to muster his oarsmen and meet him at the sound.

Reimer went about the hamlet, rousing his men, and the little party of mortals gathered at the landing, where the dwarf stood alone, silhouetted against the moonlit waters of the fjord. The ferry rocked heavily in its slip, water lapping at its gunwales as if it were fully loaded, although nothing could be seen on its broad deck but a few chests.

The oarsmen shook their heads in bafflement, but on a sign from the dwarf they took their places and strained at the oars, and the ferry moved ponderously toward the streak of white that marked the snowbound northern shore.

When the ferry was berthed at the far landing, there was a drumming, as if of myriad quick footsteps, and the ferry trembled and rose in the water. Then the dwarf ordered the boatmen to return to the southern shore for another load.

The ferry made many more such trips that night, each time bearing an invisible cargo across the sound.

At last, as the moon sank toward the horizon and the ferry was unburdened once again, the dwarf called a halt. He asked Reimer and his men to carry ashore the chests, which still littered the deck of the ferry, and when the men had set them on the shingle, he opened one. It brimmed with treasure, cobwebbed and grimy but priceless, and the dwarf scooped a handful of gold from the chest for each of the men. Then he pulled his red cap from his pocket and held it out to Reimer. "I wish you to see what you have carried. Put on the cap, and you will understand why I have asked you to go to this trouble."

Reimer donned it, then murmured an oath. For what the cap revealed was awesome and woeful. Where earlier he had seen only the slick black rocks of the shingle and the snowfields beyond, now the landscape was dense with dwarfs. They gathered in ragged knots, huddled together by pairs, or slumped alone and dejected in the snow.

Shaken, Reimer returned the magical cap, and the dwarf regarded the mortal gravely. "Our time is up," said the dwarf sadly, "and we must leave the realm of mortals. We do not know where we will settle, but we will remember your kindness through all our wanderings."

Then the little man turned and trudged off through the snow. And from the shore and the snowy meadows, Reimer heard the invisible multitudes sigh as they shouldered their burdens, an ancient and weary tribe leaving its ancestral land.

A Sampling of Dwarf Types

For all their diversity, dwarfs could be usefully classified by their activities and their relations with humanity. Some, like the brownies of Britain and the *massarioli* of Italy, were little more than servants, albeit capricious ones. Others, like the Irish leprechauns, hoarded treasure and were therefore pursued by humans. And a few, such as Scotland's sanguinary redcaps, were pursuers, not pursued; they preyed on humankind (*page 105*).

But one ancient tribe of dwarfs lived apart from men, objects of curiosity, seldom seen. These were the shy *pitikos* of the Greek isles (*below*). They were farmers, threatened each year by the hunger of migratory cranes. When the great birds darkened the sky, the foot-high *pitikos* herded their tiny cattle into caves, then took up arms and drove the flocks away.

The massariol

The jolly *massariol*, or "little farmer," of northeastern Italy tended horses and cows, fattening them on the finest grain and braiding their manes or tails on Fridays. When not in the pastures, he often could be found in the farmhouse ogling pretty young women, for the *massariol* was an ever-hopeful ladies' man.

The Kobold

Helpful if properly treated, the *Kobold* of northern Europe was a cheerful domestic devoted to mortal hearths and homes. But he caused complete chaos if he was ignored or abused by his chosen human family.

The cluricaune

A solitary sort, the Irish cluricaune spent most of his time drinking alone in the household wine cellar (and scaring off dishonest servants who tried to do likewise). Though usually drunk, he was always nattily dressed.

The leprechaun

A gold hoarder and a cobbler, the Irish leprechaun could be traced by the ceaseless rat-a-tat-tat of his hammer. Sometimes he was caught, but no mortal ever succeeded in stealing his fabled gold. He would cleverly distract his captors, then disappear in a wink.

The monaciello

The *monaciello*, or "little monk," of Naples had the unmonk-like habits of guarding hidden treasure and, when he was feeling mischievous, of pinching people and stealing their clothes. But he could enrich anyone lucky or tricky enough to steal his prized scarlet hat, for he would trade from his hoard to regain it.

The Wichtlein

For play, the *Wichtlein* dwelling in German mines rained down showers of rocks on human laborers, who took the dwarf's presence as a sign of abundant ore. The *Wichtlein* also put on noisy shows of hard work, accomplishing nothing, to warn miners of coming catastrophe.

The boggart

When abused, the usually peaceable household brownie of Scotland turned into a boggart, a renegade who was less mischievous than he was downright evil. He wrecked his humans' house; he stole the children's bread and butter and knocked their porridge to the floor; in extreme cases, he terrorized entire neighborhoods. And those who sought to avoid his torments by moving to new districts would find the move in vain. The boggart traveled with his household, hiding in crocks or butter churns.

The redcap

The terrifying redcap of the
Scottish Border country — also
known as red comb, powrie,
dunter or bloody cap — inhabited abandoned castles where
violence had once been done,
climbing to the tops of the
towers to attack unsuspecting
travelers. His name derived
from his penchant for dyeing
his cap in the warm blood of
his victims. It was thought
that he could be defeated by
the image of the Cross: If a
mortal held a Crucifix or a
cross-handled sword before
the redcap's eyes, the creature
would disappear, leaving only
a talon-like fingernail behind.

Chapter Four

Haunters of Hearth and Hayloft

One morning, a sexton in a market town on the Danish island of Samso discovered that the church he tended had been visited while he slept. The signs were few and faint, but to the old man, who knew every creaking board in the well-worn floor, every bubble and blemish in the leaded windowpanes, they were clear enough.

Stiff with age, he had become faltering in his duties. Although he swept and dusted as best he could, cobwebs darkened crannies he could no longer reach, and the church's bronze bell, so assiduously polished in bygone days, had grown dull with verdigris. But that morning, every corner of the whitewashed walls sparkled in the sunshine spilling through the windows, and the strips of floor beneath the pews, where puffs of dust sometimes escaped the old man's broom, gleamed as bright as ever. The sexton stepped out the door into the market square to gaze up at the bell tower, and he saw that even the bell had been restored to its old luster. Shaking his head in bafflement, he went back inside and climbed to the loft beneath the steeple. That room had been littered with old prayer books and peppered with mouse droppings, but now the books stood against the walls in neat stacks and the floor was pristine. It seemed, however, that a new creature had taken up residence: In a corner lay a mass of greasy rags, dimpled in the center as if a dog had made its bed there.

None of this made any sense to the sexton, although he spent the next few hours pondering the situation. At noon, shrugging as if to set the mystery aside, he rose and made ready to toll the midday hour. He climbed to the loft again, grasped the bellpull that dangled through a hole in the ceiling and gave it a firm tug. To his dismay, the bell overhead was silent, although it swung easily in its cradle. Painfully, he scaled the ladder that led to a trap door in the ceiling and pushed his way up into the bell tower. He stooped and peered under the lip of the bell, and there he discerned the cause of its silence: The clapper was wrapped in the same greasy cloth that was heaped in the loft. This was a curious clue—a prank quite at odds with the diligent labors done elsewhere in the church.

More puzzled than ever, the sexton crept beneath the bell to free the clapper. When he emerged with the rags, he glanced at the narrow streets and steep-pitched roofs below him, half-expecting to see a crowd of lads looking up and guffawing at the outcome of their mischief. He was astonished to find himself watched from much closer quarters. A diminutive visage, wearing a look of apology, confronted the old man across the crown of the bell. Above a fringe of white beard, the face was wrinkled and brown as a dried apple, and the eyes were dark as raisins. The sexton now knew what manner of visitor had eased his old age. It was a nisse, one of a breed of solitary dwarfs who made their homes in mortal houses, barns and public buildings throughout Denmark and Norway. Quite clearly, the dwarf had wrapped the clapper in rags to keep the bell silent while he gave it a vigorous polishing during the night.

Having shown himself to the sexton — evidently by way of contrition for failing to set the bell aright when the cleaning was done — the nisse disappeared. But the sexton was very pleased, and not just at the prospect of having such an able helper in residence. As a man nearing the end of his years, he possessed a lively sense of history, and he felt himself to be a privileged link to an earlier time, when the dwarf race had lived side-by-side with the peasantry. That had been long ago, but not so long as to fade from mortal memory — or to entirely dispel the pall of gloom cast over the countryside when the tribes of little folk departed.

No one was sure where the dwarf multitudes had fled when their relations with humanity soured and they left their ancestral haunts. Perhaps they retreated to regions unknown to mortal geographers. In any event, farmfolk sometimes speculated that they might return. Such hopes were based chiefly on the continuing presence of solitary dwarfs in mortal precincts and on the strength of their ties to humans. In fact, relations between mortals and the remnant population of little folk were closer than had ever been the case in earlier days. The dwarfs had become spirits of the hearth and the barnyard, aiding housewives, farmers and hired hands, and magically guarding the prosperity of the household, usually for a paltry payment of food. A church did not often attract such a tenant, but this one presented a particular opportunity for a dwarf in search of work — and indeed, the nisse continued his nightly labors until the end of the sexton's days.

The departure of the dwarf tribes altered Europe's society of races in more ways than one. In part it was a diaspora, and it sprinkled dwarfs across the face of Europe, even in lands that had not known their forebears. No longer a unified people with shared customs and quirks, these latter-day dwarfs took on local peculiarities in manner and appearance. They were known, as well, by a plethora of names — among them, *nisse* in Denmark and Norway, *tomte* in Sweden, *Kobold* in Germany, and *brownie*, *bwbach* and *bwca* in the British Isles. In Normandy, the helpful dwarfs who watched over children and tended the horses were called *lutins*; in Russia, similar domestic spirits were known as *domoviye*. A Swiss dwarf called *napfhans* aided the household in return for a daily bowl of cream, and in Spain, far from the former range of tribal dwarfs, dwarfish sprites known as *duende* made their homes within the whitewashed walls of peasant cottages.

Diverse as they were, all of these beings shared a history of retreat before vigorous humanity, followed by accommodation with the unwitting victors, and all bore the marks of their servile condition. Chief among those signs was a fierce loyalty to individual mortals. In the old days, when dwarfs and humans shared the countryside as separate peoples, dwarfs' beneficence ordinarily was general and impersonal, bestowed on entire villages or districts rather than on single favored mortals. Dwarfs' loyalties lay with their own kind.

But the dwarfs remaining after the retreat inhabited a world that was no longer their own. Living as guests in mortal dwellings, they felt a need to curry favor by vigorously defending the interests of the proprietors. Stories abound of brownies and nisses who punished sluggish maidservants and thieving hired hands, all to the profit of the master of the house. Ancestral dwarfs had punished mortal iniquity, too, but they had meted out dispassionate justice from a position of power; their descendants' anger was a bid for mortal good will – an act of weakness.

It was another sign of dwarfs' diminished state as a people that their individual loyalties brought them into conflict with one another. When the interests of their human masters were at odds, dwarfs often acted as those masters' henchmen. In Denmark, for instance, the nisse of a farm that was running short of grain might steal from a neighboring farm. If that farm, too, was tended by a vigilant nisse, the result was usually a vulgar scuffle. Sometimes, though, the quarreling dwarfs called on their ancient powers of magic, and then the battle was spectacular and terrifying.

The Danes tell of a dispute sparked during a season of drought, when the fertile fields of Jutland grew parched and brown. Nisses on adjacent farms, fearing a winter of scarcity, grew thievish, each plundering the other's storerooms by night. At first, neither dwarf was suspicious, although they soon found that their efforts brought no profit to their farms: The stocks of grain seemed to dwindle even as the nisses labored to supplement them. But one night they met in the lane, each heavily burdened with loot. Instantly, they sprang from beneath their loads and belabored each other with furious blows. When the skirmish was over, one dwarf lay bruised and exhausted in the dust, his gray robe torn and his red cap knocked askew. The victor staggered home, groaning beneath a doubled load.

The defeated nisse dragged himself back to his farm and, taking a most unusual step, slipped into the hired man's shed at the back of the stable to rouse him. The man sat up with a jolt; he knew that the farm harbored a nisse, but he was startled to meet the spirit face to face. The dwarf crouched by the man's cot, his face shadowed but his eyes feverishly bright. In an urgent whisper, he explained what had happened – and what would happen next.

His foe would be back to complete his revenge, the dwarf was certain, and this time the battle would be savage. For all his

Nisses, the domestic dwarfs of Scandinavia, were not above stealing to aid their human families' farms. On one occasion, the consequence was a battle between neighboring nisses, fought in the form of flaming wheels.

aid to the hired man in cleaning the stable and caring for the horses, he now asked a favor. Toward midnight the next day, he said, a fiery wagon wheel would bowl up the lane toward the barn. That would be the hostile nisse, and he himself would sally forth in the same guise—but with only eight spokes to his opponent's twelve. "Wait beside the barn door with a pitchfork," said the dwarf, "and when my foe is upon me, lunge upon him and beat out his spokes. If he is vanquished, this farm will thrive, but if I am the loser, its fortunes will slip, and without my aid you will toil as never before." The man nodded, and the dwarf disappeared into the shadows.

The next night the man waited at the edge of the farmyard, pitchfork in hand, peering anxiously down the lane. The air was still and silent, and the evening star glowed above a dark fringe of woods. Then a spark of orange appeared at the crest of a rise, traversed the flank of a hill and vanished behind a screen of trees. Suddenly it lurched into full view at the bottom of the lane. It was a blazing wagon wheel, trailing flames and throwing off a shower of sparks as it bounded over the ruts toward the barn.

At that instant, a patch of brilliance flared on the ground before the barn door, as if a fire had broken out within. Then, all in flames, a smaller wheel, with eight spokes, sped out the door and across the farmyard to intercept the intruder. The wheels met with a splintering crash. Flame billowed, and the smaller wheel toppled onto its hub, still spinning lazily, two of its spokes broken away.

The larger wheel reeled and wobbled from the impact, and the hired man saw his chance. He sprang from the shadows and into the storm of heat and glare. Wielding the pitchfork with all his strength, he cut and thrust at the twelve-spoked wheel, stripping away spoke after spoke.

From behind the man sounded the crackle of an angry blaze, and the smaller wheel, upright again, whirled past him and crashed into the stricken intruder, sending it spinning across the farmyard like a top. Abruptly the larger wheel regained its composure and vaulted into the air. It shot skyward like a meteor returning to its

source, dwindled to a point of orange among the blue-white stars and vanished. And when the hired man's wondering gaze at last returned to earth, the second fiery wheel had disappeared as well.

But staccato panting sounded from just inside the barn. There stood the nisse, his white hair tousled and his clothes streaked with soot, grinning broadly. After a moment, he scampered away into the dark recesses of the barn, and the hired man never met him again. But the granary stayed full even in the leanest years, while the fortunes of the neighboring farm slipped steadily; its nisse never returned.

Although the nisses' loyalty to their human families was founded on self-interest, the ties could take deeper roots—a natural result of the intimate conditions under which mortals and their dwarfish helpers lived. For example, one Scottish brownie served the lovely daughter of a laird not just by laying out her dresses and tidying her wardrobe, but also by acting as her confidant. Whenever the girl grew pensive or moody in her chamber overlooking the moor, she called softly into the fireplace. Soon one of the stones on the cold hearth would grate aside, and the dwarf, knee-high, clad in brown and so heavily bearded that in all of his face only his eyes had expression, would step into view.

During each visit, as the brownie sat quietly on an andiron, the girl would tell him of the strapping lads who came daily to court her. If she puzzled over their relative merits, the brownie would counsel her in a voice that rumbled soothingly. When her favor settled for a time on one or another of her swains, the brownie carried messages for her. She thrust them into his silky-furred fist as he retreated into the hearth, pulling the stone back into place behind him, and her lovers all marveled at how quickly her answers to their letters arrived under their doors.

At last the girl made her choice, and the maidservants and menservants were amazed at the swiftness with which the wedding preparations went forward. Guest rooms overnight lost their patina of dust and odor of mildew, the silver shed its tarnish, and the crystal took on new sparkle. As the day drew near and the cooks set to work baking cakes and concocting dainties, they found that invisible help was available. If flour needed to be sifted or cream churned to butter, the cooks had only to leave it overnight on the kitchen benches and the work would be done. Those among the servants who knew of the brownie winked at one another, amused by the spirit's show of favor.

After the girl had begun her new life as a married woman, living with her young husband in his family's stronghold, her need for the brownie's services was less. But his devotion was unstinting. He had occasion to show it when the pain of labor seized her at the birth of her first child. All that day, a gale had been raging, and the stream that ran between the stronghold and the village where the local midwife lived was in violent flood. The husband, unwilling to leave his wife's side, sent a stableboy to fetch the old woman. But the boy delayed in saddling his mare, reluctant to venture into the elements and brave the stream's turbulence.

As he dawdled, rubbing his mount with a wisp of straw and crooning in its ear, the laird's own dapple gray stallion leaped from its stall and clattered toward the stable door. It bore neither saddle nor bridle, but the lad, as he tugged the mare out of the way, saw a small brown figure clinging to its back. The brownie's fists were buried in its mane, and he leaned forward to shout in its ear, urging the horse on.

It was well for his mistress that he had taken matters into his own hands. For when he splashed up to the castle gates with the old woman clinging to his narrow shoulders and the great horse steaming from its exertions, the lad still loitered among the stalls. Not guessing the helpful spirit's errand, the boy had continued his lazy preparations. When the brownie returned his mount to the stable, the sight of the idle lad, heedless of his mistress's need, enraged him. He sprang from the horse, seized a bridle that hung on a nail, and thrashed the cowering boy until his face and arms were a map of welts.

Brownies, nisses and their kin were the best of domestics, as hard-working and loyal as any mortal master ever wished, but they were by no means domesticated. Servile though they were, their kinship to the potent dwarfs of old was unmistakable. Like their ancestors, they were most active by night, and although the signs of their presence were plain enough, they were a reclusive lot, sometimes calling on their kind's ancient power of invisibility to elude mortal eyes. They displayed other flashes of the old dwarfish powers, too,

most often in the form of gentle mischief.

Yet even playful magic could be disruptive, and it served to remind mortals of the difference between their dwarf helpers and other workers. For all their loyalty, these dwarfs were an unruly and unpredictable lot. Perhaps their delight in unsettling their mortal masters reflected an unease in their position. Descendants of a proud race, they were not disposed always to smile and do their duty.

Often, the victim of a dwarf's mischief was not a member of the family but a visitor, for, territorial as they were, dwarf helpers tended to dislike strangers. One Welsh bwbach, a good-natured dwarf whose chief service was to churn any cream that the housewife left out overnight, chose a Baptist minister as his butt.

The preacher was a distant relative of the family and had come to stay for a month. Lean and dour, he looked with disapproval on the gambols of the children, the tolerant manner of their parents and the cheerful disarray of the farmhouse. His presence had a blighting effect. The children played in whispers, fearful of disturbing the visitor in his meditation or rest, and ale disappeared from the dinner table. The bwbach, watching from the shadows of the scullery, saw the changes and decided to intercede. Soon he struck his first blow.

The preacher's bedtime prayers were lengthy and fervent. One night, as the man knelt in his nightshirt, his hands clasped and his elbows supported on a stool, a short, sinewy arm reached from

Some household dwarfs refused to tolerate anyone who interfered with the
rhythms of their masters' homes, as a Welsh preacher once discovered: A mischief-
making bwbach drummed the meddlesome cleric right off his family's property.

under the bed and stretched like taffy until its fingers closed around a leg of the stool. The preacher broke off his prayer and stared in horror, then shut his eyes tightly and began to pray with redoubled fervor. In a flash, the arm snapped back to its former length, whipping the stool from under the preacher's elbows and pitching the man onto his chin. There was a wheeze of laughter, quickly choked off, although the preacher, bruised and trembling, could not tell where it came from. He picked himself up and climbed into bed, but he did not blow out the candle.

The next day, the dwarf struck again when the family sat down to the evening meal. The children were scrubbed and silent, and their elders stiff and circumspect—all in all, a proper dinner atmosphere by the preacher's lights. As he intoned grace, the fire irons on the hearth began to tremble and dance, clattering on the stones. But the hand that stirred them was unseen. The preacher blanched and stared. Meanwhile, the children smirked into their napkins, knowing the culprit. A moment later, the hearth was still, but the dogs sleeping beneath the table awoke, stood and shook themselves, then sat back on their haunches and began to howl. The sight or sound that agitated them was imperceptible to humans, and the preacher suspected supernatural origins. Visibly unnerved, he complained of indigestion and retired to his room.

The bwbach's goal was not simply to plague the minister but to drive him from the house, as the final act showed. Some days later, the children, playing in a flower-dappled meadow near the farmhouse, came upon the preacher lying face down in the grass in a dead faint. They prodded him until he groaned and rolled over. Recognizing them, he sat up, declared loudly that he would leave that very night and told them what had happened.

He had been striding through the grass, leafing through his hymnbook and humming his favorite melodies, when he heard footsteps behind him. The sun was at his back, and on the ground before him he saw another shadow draw even with his own. He stopped and turned, then grew faint with terror. For the figure that confronted him was his own, carrying the same hymnbook and even humming the same hymn. Perhaps, he told the children, the apparition was a fetch—a mirror image that was said to appear before a person who was about to die—but he took it instead as a sign from God that he should leave the district.

The apparition was neither, as the children guessed; rather, it was a phantom conjured by the bwbach. That night, they gathered on the doorstep to watch the preacher depart. He slung his saddlebags across his mount's bony back, said his good-bys and hefted his lanky form into the saddle. Just after their parents returned to the parlor, the children saw a small figure, a brown whirl of hair and beard, dash from the barn and vault onto the rump of the horse, crowing gleefully. The nag lurched into a gallop, and the preacher twisted around, bellowing in fear when he saw the bearded dwarf clinging to his coattails. A moment later, as the preacher's shouts faded in the distance, the dwarf ambled back up the lane and disappeared into the barn, grinning with satisfaction.

The wizardry that drove away the preacher had little real malice in it, and in truth most domestic dwarfs used their supernatural powers to sportive ends or in dealing with their own kind. But the harsh character of their ancestors still surfaced from time to time in their relations with humans, and the results could be horrifying—especially considering the dwarfs' customary good nature. One victim of an outburst of dwarfish wrath was a Norwegian hired boy who foolishly treated a nisse with the same cheerful roughness he used with his mortal comrades.

The boy was a wanderer who had found a season's work as a stablehand. During those months he and the nisse had become close companions. At night, when the boy lay on his pallet in the hayloft, pining for his native village, the nisse sometimes squatted by his pillow, his gray beard dangling nearly to the floor and his knowing old eyes luminous in the dark. He said little, but the boy was comforted. When he slept, the nisse crept about the barn, shoveling manure and feeding, watering and grooming the animals, lightening the chores the boy would face the next day.

The bond between boy and dwarf had playful moments, too. Once, after the boy had tossed forkfuls of hay from the loft to the barn floor, something struck him just behind the knees, and he tumbled face first from the loft into the hay below. He heard a chuckle, and when he had brushed the wisps of hay from his face, he saw the nisse perched at the edge of the loft.

One night it was the boy who made mischief, only to find that to a dwarf, turnabout was anything but fair play. Trudging back to the barn after the evening meal of porridge and salt fish, which he took in the main house with the family, he saw the nisse sitting on an upturned bucket in a pool of moonlight. Spread across his knees was his woolen shirt, and his meager back and neck, fleeced with snowy hair, were bent as he scrutinized the garment, picking lice from the seams and cracking them between his fingernails. A cloud swept across the moon, and the nisse looked up in irritation. "Shine on, moon, so I can see to crack my lice," he said, oblivious to the boy standing behind him.

Thinking to startle the dwarf, the boy picked up a twig, crept near and tapped him on the pallid skin of one shoulder. The nisse did not jump, as the boy expected, but slowly stood and turned, letting his shirt slip to the ground. The face that confronted the boy was not the kindly visage he was used to, but harsh and alien.

The nisse stepped close to the boy, and in his eyes the boy saw a cold glitter. When he took the boy's arm, the lad flinched, but the grasp tightened cruelly around his wrist. Effortlessly, the dwarf jerked the lad off his feet and whirled him over his head like an unwieldy slingshot, while the joints of the lad's arm popped like gunfire. Suddenly the nisse released his grasp, and his victim sailed skyward, arcing high over the barn.

Magically swift, the nisse sped in a gray blur to the far side of the barn to catch the lad and hurl him skyward again, as easily as a mortal might (continued on page 122)

Playing a Cruel
Game of Names

Much tried by the mortal world, the solitary descendants of ancient dwarf tribes were uncertain in temper and given to slyness. They sold their services for high prices when they could, as the people of Suffolk learned: In a village in that county once lived an ambitious woman, the mother of a maiden so pretty and charming that she caught the eye of the lord of the manor. Almost every day he came to linger by their humble cottage and dally with the young woman. Observing this, the mother was overcome by visions of grandeur. While her daughter blushed and the lord smiled, she praised her offspring's sweetness, her tractability, her domestic skill. Warming to the subject, the woman waxed fanciful: She announced that her daughter could spin five skeins of flax a day.

The maiden stared; the suitor raised his brows. Flax, the thread from which linen was woven, was spun from plant fibers that had first been soaked and pounded. Spinning the thread was arduous work, and few women could form a single skein a day, let alone five.

"Is this truly so?" the lord asked doubtfully.

The mother folded her arms across her ample bosom and nod-ded her head in defiance.

"Then," announced the lord, "this maiden shall be my bride. I shall make her a lady, and as a lady she shall live for a year. At the end of the year, she shall spin flax for a month, to prove her worth to me.

"And if she fails," he added as an afterthought, "I will put her to death."

A lord's word was law in those days. With no more than the gown on her back, the maid left the village and went to live in the hall. But dwarfish ears had heard the interchange, and dwarfish eyes watched her go.

The lord was as good as his word. For a year, the village maiden lived like a queen. But the day came when her husband announced that it was time for her trial. That night, the bride left her fine chamber and retreated to the scullery. There, among the pots and pans, she wept for her mother's braggadocio and for the cruel will of her husband. A scuttling noise disturbed her; the shadows of the little room clustered into a shape—a small, crooked, hairy shape. It was a dwarf. He stepped up to the young bride and offered a bargain: He would spin her flax for her, he said, and all he asked in return was that she guess his name. She might have three guesses for each day that he worked, but if she did not discover his name, she would have to pay: She would become the dwarf's

woman and
go away to
live with him.
And the dwarf grinned a goblin grin.

Because the young woman had no choice, she took the dwarf's bad bargain. Each night after that, she was shut into a tower chamber with a pile of carded flax and a spinning wheel. Each night, the dwarf nipped through the window, seized the fiber and disappeared, to return in the morning with five neatly spun skeins. Each morning the bride made her three guesses, and each morning they were the wrong guesses. As the month neared its end, the dwarf's covetous grin shone permanently on his twisted face. On the last night, he gave her a cruel pinch by way of parting, and remarked that in a few hours she would be his forever, because no mortal knew the secret names of dwarfs.

It happened that night that the lord of the manor paid a visit to his wife. When he observed with pleasure that her trial would soon be over, she began unaccountably to weep. To comfort his wife, he told her of a rare sight he had seen. In a wood near her village he had come upon a dwarf, hidden in a ravine and working at a spinning wheel. As he spun, said the husband, he sang a nonsense song.

"What did he sing?" asked the wife listlessly, after she had heard this tale. Her husband sang the song for her and slowly she began to smile.

The following morning the wife watched without comment while the dwarf crawled onto the windowsill and dropped his five skeins of flax into her tower chamber. And then, with his hands on his hips, the dwarf waited for her final three guesses of his name.

The bride raised her hand to point directly at him, tracing in the air the sign against evil, and in a loud voice she recited his own nonsense rhyme.

"Nimmy, nimmy not," she cried. "Your name is Tom Tit Tot."

It was as simple as that. With a snarl, the little goblin vanished from the window, never to be seen again. And as for the bride, she lived happily from then on, or so the story says.

*Working by night, with a bowl of porridge for pay, the household dwarfs of
Europe left morning surprises for their mortal masters—piles of washed and folded
linen, rows of shining pots and pans, scrubbed and gleaming hearthstones.*

have tossed a pine cone. Again the nisse raced around the barn ahead of his victim, to catch him and fling him skyward a third time. But this time the dwarf turned and sauntered back to the bucket and his lice-ridden shirt, not even glancing up when a soft thud sounded from the far side of the barn. The family found the lad's broken body the next day, but no one thought to suspect the genial and diligent nisse.

It was rare for nisses or any of their kin to lash out so fiercely on such trifling provocation, but their touchiness was legendary. When relations between mortals and their dwarf helpers broke down, mortals often bore little of the blame: Even the best-intentioned of mortal gestures could go awry. Any attempt to reward a domestic spirit justly for his toils was likely to drive him off. Nisses, brownies and their many equivalents did vast labors for small payments, traditionally a bowl of cream or porridge left out at night or—in some lands—only on holidays. But whenever a mortal tried to make more equitable recompense—for example, rewarding a helper with a suit of clothes, sized to fit a three-year-old child—the dwarf recoiled. Perhaps the dwarf resented being treated like an ordinary servant; perhaps he saw in the largess an attempt to

bind him to a single family or farm. Whatever the case, instances abound of brownies and nisses reacting to such unexpected rewards by leaving without further ado.

Sometimes, though, the dwarf helpers remained—after first teaching the misguided mortals the folly of their generosity. A farm in Norway was blessed with a particularly diligent nisse, whose greatest delight lay in caring for the horses. Whenever the farmer drove up to the stable, he had only to unharness the horses and stow the tack, leaving everything else to the nisse.

Like most of his kind, the nisse rarely worked within mortal view, but once the curious farmer hid in a nearby shed after unhitching a team. Through a crack in the door he saw how the nisse, his stubby legs straining, pushed open the stable door and called the horses in a faint whinny, coaxing them into their stalls. There, crooning softly, he swarmed over each animal, rubbing mud from its coat, combing tail and mane, and brushing the horse until it was glossy. He pitched hay, carried water and cleaned the stalls as well, but his chief service was hidden from the farmer's gaze: Calling on his primordial gifts, he cast a genial magic that protected the horses from disease and kept them sleek and strong even when feed ran short.

The farmer was chagrined by profiting from so much labor in return for a holiday bowl of good porridge. Sometimes he left a few of his children's castoff breeches and jackets in the nisse's corner of the hayloft, for the dwarf wore nothing but a threadbare gray cloak and a moth-eaten red stocking cap. But the nisse spurned the gifts; the next morning, without fail, they lay in the barnyard, patterned with small, muddy footprints where the dwarf had trampled them. Even though they had been rejected, the farmer decided to tempt the nisse with a finer offering.

At market one day, he bought a scrap of supple white leather, and when he reached home he told his wife to fashion it into a pair of child's breeches. On Christmas Eve, while his wife cooked the nisse's holiday porridge, pale with cream and heavily sugared, the farmer fetched the breeches from the chest where they were stored. He carried porridge pot and breeches to the hayloft and placed them beside the whorl of straw that marked the nisse's bed.

The next day, the family drove by sleigh to church and merrily toured nearby farms. When they drew up before the stable, snow had begun to fall. The farmer bundled his wife and children indoors, then unhitched the sleigh and dragged it into its shed, leaving the horses snorting in the cold. He gave them no further thought as he followed his family indoors and drew close to the warmth of the fire.

As night fell, his wife bustled and clattered in the kitchen and the children romped near the hearth, but soon another sound penetrated the farmer's comfortable reverie: the pitiful neighing of horses suffering in the cold. He hurried out the door into the bluster of the storm and saw the team still standing where he had left it; the horses' backs were now mantled with snow, and the animals stomped and shivered in an effort to stay warm. Cursing the nisse, he led the team through the drifts and into the stable. There he found the dwarf, leaning against a post, his hands deep in the pockets of his new leather breeches, smiling brightly.

The man was bursting with rage. "What is the meaning of this?" he spluttered. "The horses are nearly dead of the cold."

The nisse grinned more broadly, and he spread his hands in a gesture of helplessness. "In weather so bad, with clothing so fine, how can you expect me to trouble about horses?"

The farmer was chastened, and he said nothing when, the next morning, he found the leather breeches floating beneath a skin of ice in the trough that stood before the barn. After that, the farmer never ventured to offer the nisse anything more than was customary, and the dwarf's diligence was unflagging.

Considering how readily even kindly gestures could misfire, it is no surprise that deliberate abuse could embitter a dwarf permanently. If dwarfs were ill-treated, their unease in their position as members of a servile race changed to a sense of injury, and they turned against the world of humankind forever. Many reached that sad pass not after a single offense but after repeated affronts, which drove them from family to family and at last persuaded them to forsake the mortal world.

A Welsh tale shows how it could happen. A maid at a Monmouthshire farm was the envy of the other servants, for she lay abed late and idled much of the day, yet earned the mistress's praise by doing chores enough for two. Every evening, hanks of unspun wool, hampers of un-

Such malignant dwarfs were well known in the region of England near the Scottish border—a stretch of moors, windy crags and ruined fortresses. There, herds of wild goats cropped the tough moorland grasses, the cries of curlews rang across the hills, and a sense of nameless danger hovered in the air. Solitary wayfarers crossed the borderlands at their own risk, and when they were safely gathered in company, told such travelers' tales as this:

One winter evening, a wanderer hurrying through the descending gloom strayed from the narrow path, and by nightfall he was stumbling across a stony slope, utterly lost. As he rounded the shoulder of the hill, he saw a light in the depths of a glen.

He made his way toward it and soon discerned a stone hut, with firelight showing through a window. It was no more than a shepherd's rude shelter, but when the man crouched low to slip in the entrance, he found a leaping blaze, well stoked, with fuel enough beside it for a night's warmth. Otherwise, the hut was empty, but the traveler was too weary to wonder whose hospitality he was presuming on, and he sank onto a stone to one side of the blaze.

The fire burned low, a distant owl hooted, and the traveler nodded. Suddenly a rattle of stones outside roused him. A dwarf no higher than his knee, but thickset and powerful, entered the hut. He was clad in heavy layers of hide that creaked as he perched on a stone on the opposite side of the fire, and a strip of dry moss bound his long, matted hair. He rested massive hands on his knees, showing fingernails as thick as armor plate, and he scowled at the man from beneath heavy brows.

the field. In the end the long-suffering families appealed to a magician, who summoned up a whirlwind; after its funnel had corkscrewed across the fields and out of sight over the horizon, the district was still. The wise man claimed that the wind had caught up the dwarf among its swirl of dust and leaves and set him down in a distant land.

Vexing as it was, the bwca's mischief was mild. Other dwarfs, victims of harsher treatment or by nature more vengeful, turned against the mortal world not in sadness but in rage. Their campaign against humanity was grim and relentless. Outlaw spirits, they lurked at the fringes of human settlement, harassing travelers and herdsmen, endlessly taking revenge for wrongs committed long before.

If offended by their mortal housemates, domestic dwarfs deserted, leaving behind a trail of wreckage—crumbled crockery, broken furniture and dirtied linen.

The traveler did not dare speak, but he cared even less to venture out into the night again. As the chill encroached on the dying fire, he fumbled for the kindling piled beside his stone and fed a handful into the coals The dwarf looked at him with contempt, then stood and hefted one of the huge logs that lay on his side of the blaze. It was as long and thick as a man, but the dwarf broke it effortlessly across his knee and shot the pieces into the blaze. With a heavy boot, he singled out another log from the pile and rolled it to the edge of the hearth Then he sat down again and glared at the traveler, silently challenging him to match his feat of strength.

But the man, by now thoroughly unsettled, did nothing. The fire dwindled to a bed of embers that one by one faded into darkness. Soon only the raspy breathing of the dwarf revealed his presence. Although frightened and achingly cold, the traveler dozed, and when he awoke the dwarf was visible again, outlined by the ash gray light of dawn, his hate-filled gaze still fastened on the man.

In the distance, a cock crowed, and at that faint sound the scene was transformed. Hut, cold hearth and dwarf dissolved, and the wayfarer found himself alone on the barren slope he had stumbled down the night before. Blinking, he gazed around, and his stomach turned with horror. A pace or two from him, where the dwarf had squatted, a deep ravine gaped its depths littered with human bones, smashed like crockery. The man saw that if he had answered the dwarf's unspoken challenge and crossed to the far side of the fire to pick up the log, he would have tumbled to his death, following a cruel harvest of other victims, less wary than he.

When the traveler sought refuge at a crofter's cottage that morning, the family told him that he had encountered a duergar, one of a breed of illusion-weaving, daylight-shunning dwarfs. And they spoke of other borderland dwarfs, even more virulent in nature, known as redcaps. Solitary haunters of ruined fortresses and the squat stone towers moorland families once used for shelter against marauders, redcaps scanned the horizon from loopholes and battlements, watching for travelers. When a mortal drew near an infested castle, the dwarf would storm from his tumble-down stronghold, his iron boots striking sparks, to ambush the wanderer and run him through with a halberd. Then, with lank gray locks swinging and eyes aglitter, the dwarf would crouch by the corpse and pull the faded red cap from his head to soak it in the wound, renewing its color with human blood.

For all their ghoulish contrast with other dwarfs, such outlaw spirits shared a common purpose with the kindly haunters of house and barn. All centered their lives on mortals; their existences were focused only by their deep loyalty to humanity or by implacable enmity. The days when dwarfs were aloof and enigmatic, their

Wary of the mortal world, mining dwarfs harked back to an age their house-dwelling, servile relatives had forgotten. They lived deep in the earth in tribes, using their ancient, ancestral skills to fashion treasures no human would ever see.

pursuits mysterious and their favor or hostility to mortals incidental to their true concerns, seemed gone forever.

There was little room, after all, for a parallel race like the dwarfs of old, going its own way and guarding its own secrets, in a Europe that by now was thoroughly tamed to the needs of mortals. Humanity had heaped up cities and webbed the landscape with roadways. And mortals were knowers as well as builders, seeing in their earthly surroundings little they could not control or comprehend. Yet there remained realms that mortals had penetrated but not mastered, where men felt themselves to be intruders, confronting forces they did not understand.

Such a realm was the underground world of mines. In the flickering glow of miners' lanterns, shadows loomed large, and furtive shapes fled from the fringe of the light. The timbers shoring up the tunnels creaked incessantly, and tiny avalanches of pebbles pattered from the tunnel ceilings. In the far reaches of dark galleries, veils of blue flame sometimes danced and shimmered, vanishing between one glance and the next. And disasters — cave-ins and explosions — could strike without warning.

Underground, mortals were on their guard for another reason: The mines were haunted by dwarfs — not the familiar spirits of house and barn but beings who possessed some of the forbidding majesty of their ancestors. Although their kin aboveground had drifted into an uneasy dependence on human beings, the dwarfs of the mines had remained tribal and aloof.

Workers of the tin mines of Cornwall knew them as knockers; in the coal mines of Wales, they were called coblynau, and in the silver mines of Bohemia the workers spoke of *Haus-schmiedlein*. The dwarfs rarely ventured into the circles of light shed by the miners' lamps, although an occasional miner claimed to have seen one, a squat, big-headed old man in drab garb, who regarded him impassively from a niche in a tunnel wall. More often, they made their presence known by rapping within hidden galleries — a sign to mortal miners that a rich vein of ore lay nearby. At times the tapping sounded more rapidly, and from all directions, as the dwarfs tried to warn the mortals of an impending cave-in. In gratitude, some miners left gifts of food or children's clothing in remote recesses of the mine. Such gifts, however, were offerings, not rewards, betokening none of the dominance mortals held over dwarfs in the upper world.

The earth had nurtured dwarfs in the earliest days of creation, and it harbored them still. Perhaps the dwarfs who aided miners were only the most visible members of a teeming population sheltering in mazy passages within the vast reaches of the nether world. Some may have dwelled in the smoky depths since the dawn of time; others no doubt were refugees, returned to their element after their bruising sojourn in the upper world. And perhaps they bide their time there still, charming mineral riches from the rocks and practicing their old arts, awaiting the day when their earth-shaping skills will once again dazzle mortals and gods alike.

The Night Workers

The farms of old Russia were home to more than farmers and animals. Even the rudest homestead was haunted by *domoviye*, shy but strong-willed dwarfs who helped with its management.

Each of the hirsute little assistants had his own jealously guarded domain. The *vasily* held sway over the horses (he was hoofed, in token of this role). The *ovinnik* dwelled in the barn, tending the livestock—or some of the livestock, at any rate: Each *ovinnik* had a favorite color and ignored beasts that lacked it. The feisty *bannik* ruled the bath—and was not above scalding humans who bathed late at night, when it was his turn.

Most important of all was the house-dwelling *domovoi*. This intensely loyal creature performed domestic chores and served as a household alarm, waking the family during a fire, groaning at the approach of plague and crying bitterly before a death. But when his masters forgot to leave him food at night or otherwise offended him, he wrecked the kitchen or, worse, deserted the family altogether, leaving it unprotected.

When sleigh bells tinkled on winter nights and dogs barked

e dark, a farmer knew his vasily was taking the horse for exercise in the snow.

Farmers kept fires in the barnyard to warm the ovinnik wh

...e went about his duties. If he built his own fire in the barn, disaster might result.

AUSTIN·1984

After his own bath, the wise peasant left water and a brush fo

...e bathhouse *bannik* and the forest sprites that were sometimes invited to join him.

AUSTIN·1984

Bad language, poor food or human curiosity enraged the

...omestic domovoi, luring him from behind the stove to topple tables and benches.

Picture Credits

The sources for the illustrations in this book are shown below. When known, the artist's name precedes the picture source.

Cover: Arthur Rackham, from *Fairy Tales of the Brothers Grimm*, Constable and Company, 1909, by permission of Barbara Edwards, courtesy Mary Evans Picture Library, London. 1-5: Artwork by James C. Christensen. 6, 7: Artwork by Kinuko Y. Craft. 10-14: Artwork by Wayne Anderson. 16, 17: Artwork by Kinuko Y. Craft. 18: Artwork by Winslow Pinney Pels. 20, 21: Artwork by Kinuko Y. Craft. 22: Artwork by Winslow Pinney Pels. 24: Artwork by Chris Van Allsburg. 26: Artwork by Wayne Anderson. 28, 29: Artwork by John Jude Palencar. 30: Artwork by Wayne Anderson. 32-39: Artwork by Gary Kelley. 40-43: Artwork by Rallé. 46, 47: Artwork by Wayne Anderson. 48, 49: Artwork by Rallé. 51: Artwork by Wayne Anderson. 52-58: Artwork by Winslow Pinney Pels. 60-62: Artwork by Kinuko Y. Craft. 64-71: Artwork by John Howe. 72-75: Artwork by James C. Christensen. 78: Artwork by Wayne Anderson. 80, 81: Artwork by Sharleen Collicott. 83: Artwork by Mark Langeneckert. 84: Artwork by Wayne Anderson. 87: Artwork by Pauline Ellison. 88, 89: Artwork by John Howe. 92, 93: Artwork by John Jude Palencar. 94, 95: Artwork by James C. Christensen. 98-105: Artwork by Wayne Anderson. 106-114: Artwork by Mark Langeneckert. 117-121: Artwork by Christopher Wormell. 122-127: Artwork by James C. Christensen. 128: Noel Pocock, from *Grimm's Fairy Tales*, Oxford University Press, 1926, courtesy Brüder-Grimm-Museum, Kassel, photographed by Carl Eberth. 130-137: Artwork by Alicia Austin. 142-144: Artwork by James C. Christensen.

Bibliography

Aldington, Richard, and Delano Ames, transls., *New Larousse Encyclopedia of Mythology*. London: The Hamlyn Publishing Group, 1974.

Arrowsmith, Nancy, with George Moorse, *A Field Guide to the Little People*. New York: Pocket Books, 1977.*

Asbjørnsen, Peter Christen, and Jørgen Moe, *Norwegian Folk Tales*. Transl. by Pat Shaw and Carl Norman. New York: Pantheon Books, 1982.

Boucher, Alan, transl., *Elves, Trolls and Elemental Beings*. Reykjavik: Iceland Review Library, 1977.

Briggs, Katharine:
Abbey Lubbers, Banshees & Boggarts. An Illustrated Encyclopedia of Fairies. New York: Pantheon Books, 1979.*
An Encyclopedia of Fairies: Hobgoblins, Brownies, Bogies, and Other Supernatural Creatures. New York: Pantheon Books, 1976.*
The Personnel of Fairyland. Detroit: Singing Tree Press, 1971.
The Vanishing People: Fairy Lore and Legends. New York: Pantheon Books, 1978.

Bringsværd, Tor Åge, *Phantoms and Fairies from Norwegian Folklore*. Transl. by Pat Shaw Iversen. Oslo: Johan Grundt Tanum Forlag, no date.*

Byfield, Barbara Ninde, *The Glass Harmonica: A Lexicon of the Fantastical*. New York: Macmillan, 1967.

Choate, Florence, and Elizabeth Curtis, compilers, *The Little People of the Hills*. New York: Harcourt, Brace, 1928.

Christiansen, Reidar, ed., *Folktales of Norway*. Transl. by Pat Shaw Iversen. Chicago: The University of Chicago Press, 1964.

Cimo, Shirley, *Piskies, Spriggans, and Other Magical Beings: Tales from the Droll-Teller*. New York: Thomas Y. Crowell, 1980.

Craigie, W. A., *The Icelandic Sagas*. Millwood, New York: Kraus Reprint Company, 1975 (reprint of 1913 edition).*

Crossley-Holland, Kevin, *The Norse Myths*. New York: Pantheon Books, 1980.*

D'Arbois de Jubainville, Henry, *The Irish Mythological Cycle and Celtic Mythology*. Transl. by Richard Irvine Best. Dublin: Hodges, Figgis & Company, 1903.

Davidson, Hilda R. Ellis, *Gods and Myths of Northern Europe*. New York: Penguin Books, 1982.

Deane, Tony, and Tony Shaw, *The Folklore of Cornwall*. Totowa, New Jersey: Rowman and Littlefield, 1975.

Dorson, Richard M., ed., *Folktales Told around the World*. Chicago: The University of Chicago Press, 1975.

Evans-Wentz, W. Y., *The Fairy-Faith in Celtic Countries*. Secaucus, New Jersey: University Books, 1966.

Gillespie, George T., *A Catalogue of Persons Named in German Heroic Literature (700-1600), Including Named Animals and Objects and Ethnic Names*. Oxford, England: Clarendon Press, 1973.

Gimmelsberger, Erwin, *Salzburger Zwerge*. Salzburg, Austria: Stadtverein Salzburg, 1972.

Green, Roger Lancelyn, *Myths of the Norsemen*. Harmondsworth, England: Puffin Books, 1980.

Grimm, Jacob, *Teutonic Mythology*. Vols. 1 and 2. Transl. by James Steven Stallybrass. Gloucester, Massachusetts: Peter Smith, 1976 (reprints of 1883 editions). *

Grimm, Jakob Ludwig Karl, and Wilhelm Karl Grimm:
The German Legends of the Brothers Grimm. Vol. 1. Ed. and transl. by Donald Ward. Philadelphia: Institute for the Study of Human Issues, 1981.
Household Stories from the Collection of the Brothers Grimm. Transl. by Lucy Crane. Ann Arbor, Michigan: University Microfilms, 1966 (reprint of 1882 edition).
Sixty Fairy Tales of the Brothers Grimm. Transl by Mrs. Edgar Lucas. New York: Weathervane Books, 1979

Haining, Peter, *The Leprechaun's Kingdom*. New York: Harmony Books, 1980. *

Harward, Vernon J., Jr., *The Dwarfs of Arthurian Romance and Celtic Tradition*. Leiden, Netherlands: E. J. Brill, 1958.

Hatto, A. T., transl., *The Nibelungenlied*. Harmondsworth, England: Penguin Books, 1982.

Hoffmann, Alice S., *The Book of the Sagas*. London: Ernest-Nister, no date.

Hoffmann-Krayer, E., and Hanns Bächtold-Stäubli, *Handwörterbuch des Deutschen Aberglaubens*. Vol. 9. Berlin: Walter De Gruyter & Company, 1938/1941. *

Hollander, Lee M., transl., *The Poetic Edda*. Austin: University of Texas Press, 1962.

Jobes, Gertrude, *Dictionary of Mythology, Folklore and Symbols*. New York: The Scarecrow Press, 1962.

Keary, A., and E. Keary, *The Heroes of Asgard: Tales from Scandinavian Mythology*. New York: Mayflower Books, 1979 (reprint of 1870 edition).

Keightley, Thomas, *The World Guide to Gnomes, Fairies, Elves and Other Little People*. New York: Avenel Books, 1978.

Lattimore, Richmond, transl., *The Iliad of Homer*. Chicago: The University of Chicago Press, 1973.

Leach, Henry Goddard, ed., *A Pageant of Old Scandinavia*. Princeton, New Jersey: Princeton University Press, 1946.

Lindow, John, *Swedish Legends and Folktales*. Berkeley: University of California Press, 1978.

MacCulloch, John Arnott:
Medieval Faith and Fable. Folcroft, Pennsylvania: Folcroft Library Editions, 1973 (reprint of 1932 edition).
The Mythology of All Races: Eddic. Vol. 2. New York: Cooper Square, 1964

Mackenzie, Donald A., *Teutonic Myth and Legend*. Boston: Longwood Press, 1978 (reprint of 1934 edition).

Mac Manus, Diarmuid, *Irish Earth Folk*. New York: The Devin-Adair Company, 1959. *

MacRitchie, David, *Fians, Fairies and Picts*. London: Norwood Editions, 1974.

Mandel, Jerome, and Bruce A. Rosenberg, eds., *Medieval Literature and Folklore Studies*. New Brunswick, New Jersey: Rutgers University Press, no date.

Map, Walter *De Nugis Curialium (Courtiers' Trifles)*. Transl. by Frederick Tupper and Marbury Bladen Ogle. London: Chatto & Windus, 1924.

Meyers, Fritz, *Riesen und Zwerge am Niederrhein: Ihre Spuren in Sage, Märchen, Geschichte und Kunst*. Duisburg, Germany: Verlag Fachtechnik + Mercator-Verlag, 1980.

Olenius, Elsa, compiler, *Great Swedish Fairy Tales*. Transl. by Holger Lundbergh. New York: Delacorte Press/Seymour Lawrence, 1978.

Opie, Iona, and Peter Opie, *The Classic Fairy Tales*. New York: Oxford University Press 1974.

Oxenstierna, Eric Graf, *The World of the Norsemen*. Transl. by Janet Sondheimer. London: Weidenfeld and Nicolson, 1967.

Picard, Barbara Leonie:
German Hero-Sagas and Folk-Tales. London: Oxford University Press, 1975.
Tales of the Norse Gods and Heroes. London: Oxford University Press, 1980.

Piø, Iørn, *Nissen*. Copenhagen: Gyldendal, 1980.

Piø, Iørn, Gustav Henningsen and Birgitte Rørbye, "Folklore Studies in Denmark, 1953-1973" (DFS-Translations No. 2). Copenhagen: Danish Folklore Archives, 1974.

Piø, Iørn, and Johannes Knudsen, transls., *The Nisse: Traditional Danish Farm-Goblin*. Copenhagen: Gyldendals Forlag, 1980.

Schlauch, Margaret, transl., *The Saga of the Volsungs: The Saga of Ragnar Lodbrok, Together with the Lay of Kraka*. New York: The American-Scandinavian Foundation, 1930.

Sikes, Wirt, *British Goblins: Welsh Folk-Lore, Fairy Mythology, Legends and Traditions*. Wakefield, England: EP Publishing, 1973. *

Simpson, Jacqueline:
Everyday Life in the Viking Age. London: B. T. Batsford, 1967.
Icelandic Folktales and Legends. Berkeley: University of California Press, 1972. *

Simpson, Jacqueline, transl., *The Northmen Talk: A Choice of Tales from Iceland*. London: Phoenix House, 1965.

Spence, Lewis, *British Fairy Origins*. Wellingborough, England: The Aquarian Press, 1981.

Squire, Charles, *Celtic Myth and Legend Poetry and Romance*. North Hollywood, California: Newcastle Publishing, 1975.

Sturluson, Snorri, *The Prose Edda*. Transl. by Arthur Gilchrist Brodeur. New York: The American-

Scandinavian Foundation, 1967 (reprint of 1916 edition). *

Terry, Patricia, transl., *Poems of the Vikings: The Elder Edda.* Indianapolis: Bobbs-Merrill, 1969.

Thorpe, Lewis, transl., *Gerald of Wales: The Journey through Wales and the Description of Wales.* Harmondsworth, England: Penguin Books, 1980.

Tietze-Conrat, Erika, *Dwarfs and Jesters in Art.* London: Phaidon Press, 1957.

Tolkien, Christopher, transl., *The Saga of King Heidrek the Wise.* London: Thomas Nelson and Sons, 1960.

Turville-Petre, E.O.G., *Myth and Religion of the North: The Religion of Ancient Scandinavia.* New York: Holt, Rinehart and Winston, 1964.

Wagner, Wilhelm, *Romances and Epics of Our Northern Ancestors: Norse, Celt and Teuton.* London: Norrœena Society, 1906.

Titles marked with an asterisk were especially helpful in the preparation of this volume.

Acknowledgments

The editors are particularly indebted to John Dorst, consultant, for his help in the preparation of this volume. The editors also thank the following persons and institutions: American Folklife Center, Library of Congress, Washington, D.C.; François Avril, Curator, Département des Manuscrits, Bibliothèque Nationale, Paris; Barbara Edwards, Hampshire, England; Antonio Faeti, Università degli Studi, Bologna; Dieter Gleisberg, Director, Museum der Bildenden Künste, Leipzig; Marielies Göpel, Archiv für Kunst und Geschichte, West Berlin; Klaus Haenel, Leiter der Handschriften Abteilung, Universitätsbibliothek, Göttingen; Claus Hansmann, Stockdorf; Dieter Hennig, Brüder-Grimm-Museum, Kassel; Gustav Henningsen, Research Director, Danish Folklore Archives, Copenhagen; Christine Hofmann, Bayerische Staatsgemäldesammlungen, Munich; Virginia Allan Jensen, International Children's Book Service, Copenhagen; Heidi Klein, Bildarchiv Preussischer Kulturbesitz, West Berlin; Roland Klemig, Bildarchiv Preussischer Kulturbesitz, West Berlin; Kunsthistorisches Institut, Universität, Bonn; Felix J. Oinas, Professor Emeritus, Slavic Languages and Literature, Indiana University, Bloomington; Paola Pallottino, Università degli Studi, Bologna; Italo Pileri, Rome; Iørn Piø, Research Director, Danish Folklore Archives, Copenhagen; Beatrice Premoli, Museo Nazionale delle Arti e Tradizioni Popolari, Rome; Justin Schiller, New York; Françoise Viatte, Curator, Cabinet des Dessins, Musée du Louvre, Paris; Leonie von Wilkins, Germanisches Nationalmuseum, Nuremberg.

Chief Series Consultant

Tristram Potter Coffin, Professor of
English at the University of Pennsylvania, is a leading authority on folklore.
He is the author or editor of numerous
books and more than one hundred articles. His best-known works are *The British Traditional Ballad in North America*, *The
Old Ball Game*, *The Book of Christmas Folklore* and *The Female Hero*.

This volume is one of a series that is based
on myths, legends and folk tales.